CW01650077

WORKBOOK 1

prepared for the course team by norma sherratt, david goldblatt, maureen mackintosh and kath woodward

This publication forms part of an Open University course DD100 *An Introduction to the Social Sciences: Understanding Social Change*. Details of this and other Open University courses can be obtained from the Course Reservations Centre, PO Box 724, The Open University, Milton Keynes MK7 6ZS, United Kingdom: tel. +44 (0)1908 653231, e-mail ces-gen@open.ac.uk

Alternatively, you may visit the Open University website at http://www.open.ac.uk where you can learn more about the wide range of courses and packs offered at all levels by the Open University.

To purchase this publication or other components of Open University courses, contact Open University Worldwide Ltd, The Berrill Building, Walton Hall, Milton Keynes MK7 6AA, United Kingdom: tel. +44 (0)1908 858785; fax +44 (0)1908 858787; e-mail ouwenq@open.ac.uk; website http://www.ouw.co.uk

The Open University
Walton Hall, Milton Keynes
MK7 6AA

First published 2000

This text has been printed on paper produced in Sweden from wood from managed forests using an elemental chlorine-free bleaching process. It has been stated as being environmentally friendly by the Swedish Association for the Protection of Nature.

Edited, designed and typeset by the Open University.

Printed by The Bath Press, Bath.

ISBN 0 7492 7761 0

1.1

21861B/dd100wb1i1.1

Contents

Introduction **5**

Block overview 5

Key questions 6

Key skills 7

Assessing Block 1 8

1 Questions of identity **10**

1.1 Identity. What is it? 10

1.2 Constructing social science arguments 12

1.3 Sources of identity: writing skills 14

1.4 Social science and the circuit of knowledge 16

2 Identity and gender **21**

2.1 Chapter 2. What's it about? 22

2.2 Gender differences in educational achievement: working with numbers 23

2.3 Murphy and Elwood: constructing a social science argument 27

3 Identity, inequality and social class **30**

3.1 Getting orientated: economics and identity 31

3.2 How unequal are we? Using numerical data 34

3.3 Understanding social class 36

3.4 The decline of old certainties: the construction of an argument 38

4 Identity and nation **42**

4.1 Where do you come from? Place, culture and identity 42

4.2 Concepts and theories: states, nations, nation-states 46

4.3 Reading visual evidence 50

4.4 The argument of Chapter 4: how has it been constructed? 55

4.5 Using the course themes: problems of Englishness 58

5 Consolidation and reflection **60**

6 Study skills: using tutorials, the phone and self-help groups **62**

7 Assessing Block 1 **64**

7.1 Frequently asked questions about essay writing for your TMAs 64

7.2 Preparing to write an essay 65

7.3 TMA 01 67

Appendix: process and command words in essay questions **71**

Acknowledgements **73**

Study skills index **75**

The DD100 course team

John Allen, *Senior Lecturer in Geography*

Penny Bennett, *Editor*

Pam Berry, *Compositor*

Simon Bromley, *Senior Lecturer in Government*

David Calderwood, *Project Controller*

Elizabeth Chaplin, *Tutor Panel*

Giles Clark, *Co-publishing Advisor*

Stephen Clift, *Editor*

Allan Cochrane, *Professor of Public Policy*

Lene Connolly, *Print Buying Controller*

Graham Dawson, *Lecturer in Economics*

Lesley Duguid, *Senior Course Co-ordination Secretary*

Ross Fergusson, *Staff Tutor in Social Policy (Region 02)*

Fran Ford, *Senior Course Co-ordination Secretary*

David Goldblatt, *Co-Course Team Chair, Lecturer in Government*

Jenny Gove, *Lecturer in Psychology*

Judith Greene, *Professor of Psychology*

Montserrat Guibernau, *Lecturer in Government*

Peter Hamilton, *Lecturer in Sociology*

Celia Hart, *Picture Researcher*

David Held, *Professor of Politics and Sociology*

Susan Himmelweit, *Senior Lecturer in Economics*

Steve Hinchliffe, *Lecturer in Geography*

Gordon Hughes, *Lecturer in Social Policy*

Christina Janoszka, *Course Manager*

Pat Jess, *Staff Tutor in Geography (Region 12)*

Bob Kelly, *Staff Tutor in Government (Region 08)*

Margaret Kiloh, *Staff Tutor in Applied Social Sciences (Region 13)*

Sylvia Lay-Flurrie, *Secretary*

Siân Lewis, *Graphic Designer*

Tony McGrew, *Professor of International Relations, University of Southampton*

Hugh Mackay, *Staff Tutor in Sociology (Region 10)*

Maureen Mackintosh, *Professor of Economics*

Eugene McLaughlin, *Senior Lecturer in Applied Social Science*

Andrew Metcalf, *Senior Producer, BBC*

Gerry Mooney, *Staff Tutor in Applied Social Sciences (Region 11)*

Ray Munns, *Graphic Artist*

Kathy Pain, *Staff Tutor in Geography (Region 02)*

Clive Pearson, *Tutor Panel*

Lynne Poole, *Tutor Panel*

Norma Sherratt, *Staff Tutor in Sociology (Region 03)*

Roberto Simonetti, *Lecturer in Economics*

Dick Skellington, *Project Officer*

Brenda Smith, *Staff Tutor in Psychology (Region 12)*

Mark Smith, *Lecturer in Social Sciences*

Grahame Thompson, *Professor of Political Economy*

Ken Thompson, *Professor of Sociology*

Stuart Watt, *Lecturer in Psychology/KMI*

Andy Whitehead, *Graphic Artist*

Kath Woodward, *Co-Course Team Chair, Staff Tutor in Sociology (Region 07)*

Chris Wooldridge, *Editor*

External Assessor

Nigel Thrift, *Professor of Geography, University of Bristol*

INTRODUCTION

You will be working on Block 1 of the course for the next five weeks, with this workbook as your guide and with a whole week set aside for writing TMA 01 at the end. In a moment you will be starting on the Introduction and Chapter 1 of the book *Questioning Identity: Gender, Class, Nation*. Before this we want to spend a little time preparing you for Block 1.

Block overview

As with all your work on DD100, Block 1 includes a range of teaching materials, including: the textbook *Questioning Identity*, this workbook, audio-cassettes, and a TV programme (see Figure 1 below). As with the Introductory Block, you will need to think about how to organize your time and what route to take through the materials. The recommended route is shown in Figure 2. Please check the *Study Calendar* for TV programme broadcast times – we recognize that TV schedules and your working patterns may not coincide.

Study week	Course material	Suggested study time
4	*Workbook 1* and Book 1: *Questioning Identity: Gender, Class, Nation* Introduction Chapter 1 Audio-cassette 3, Side A	 1 hour 10½ hours 30 minutes
5	Workbook and Chapter 2	12 hours
6	Workbook and Chapter 3 *Study Skills Supplement 1: Reading Visual Images*, plus Audio-cassette 2	10 hours 2 hours
7	Workbook and Chapter 4 Afterword TV 01: *Defining Moments* Audio-cassette 3, Side B	9½ hours 1 hour 1 hour 30 minutes
8	Workbook and TMA 01 *Assignment Booklet 1* (TMA 01)	12 hours

FIGURE 1 Course materials for Block 1

FIGURE 2 Recommended study route for Block 1

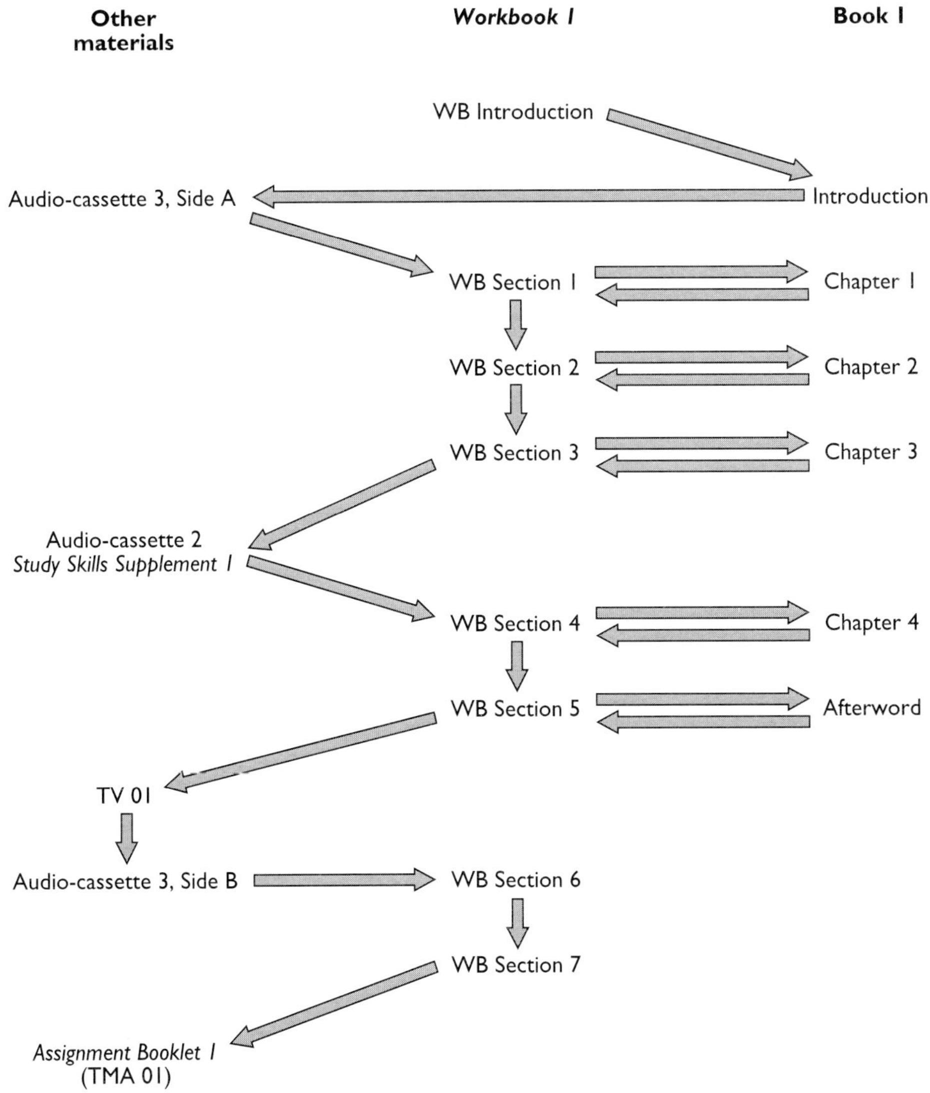

Key questions

DD100 is question driven and Block 1 is no exception. It is worth just stopping for a moment to think about the three key framing questions of the block.

1 How are identities formed?

Identities are a complex matter. They are our way of describing who we think we are, as individuals and as part of wider social groups. But how do we acquire our identities? By what processes do we come to know who we are? To what extent are our identities formed in our childhood? Do they continue to develop and change? Once established are identities fixed or do we have to constantly re-create our identities?

2 To what extent can we shape our own identities?

As you might have recognized, thinking about the formation of identity draws on the course theme of *structure and agency*. How far is what happens to us, as individuals and social groups, a result of our own wishes, intentions and decisions? To what extent are there other forces at work which are beyond our control? What might these forces be?

3 Are there uncertainties about identity in the UK?

If by identity we mean who we think we are and how others see us, then it does seem that for many people identities may not be as certain as they were in the past. All kinds of economic, social and cultural changes appear to have generated more uncertainty about who we are. The role models and experiences of earlier generations may be less reliable guides to identity today. We may have a number of different, possibly conflicting, identities presenting us with problems earlier generations never had to face.

Key skills

Alongside these framing questions of identity, your work on Block 1 will develop a key range of social science skills and study skills. These include:

- understanding the production of social science knowledge, through what we have called the *circuit of knowledge*;
- understanding how a social science argument is constructed, and the role of concepts and theories in its construction;
- learning to work with quantitative and qualitative evidence;
- learning to read visual images, including maps;
- developing some writing skills and techniques;
- developing your skills as an independent learner – in particular some techniques for using your tutor, the telephone and self-help groups to the best advantage.

In addition, as part of your work on Block 1, we will be helping you to develop the active reading and note-taking skills you began working on in the Introductory Block. Most of these skills are developed in Sections 1–4 of this workbook, in combination with your study of other course materials. Section 5 gives you an opportunity to consolidate and reflect on your work, while Section 6 picks up the independent learner skills. In Section 7 of this workbook we will turn to questions of assessment.

Assessing Block 1

At the end of your work on this block you will have an assignment (TMA 01) to send to your tutor. The questions set for the assignment will be different each year, but they will always be related closely to the work you have been doing in the workbook. Each year the question will be about identity and comes in two parts. The first part will ask you to show the progress you have made in developing one of the key social science skills: understanding how social science arguments are constructed. The second part will give you an opportunity to explore some of the key framing questions and debates of Block 1.

▶ **You might find it useful to have a quick look at *Assignment Booklet 1* (which contains TMA 01) for this year before you start work on Block 1, so that you have some idea of what you are looking for before you begin your study of *Questioning Identity* and this workbook.**

You already have quite a lot to go on to guide your reading of Block 1: keep in mind the three framing questions and the first key skill, the production of knowledge in the social sciences. It might be useful to keep in mind the grid below as you work through Block 1 as a way of collecting your thoughts on these issues from across the four main chapters of *Questioning Identity*.

▶ **Now read Kath Woodward's Introduction to *Questioning Identity* and listen to Audio-cassette 3, Side A: *Block 1 Overview*. Then return to this point in the workbook.**

Framing questions of Block 1

	Chapter 1	Chapter 2	Chapter 3	Chapter 4
How are identities formed?				
What control do we have over our identities?				
Uncertainties about identity. Evidence of diverse identities.				
How is social science knowledge produced?				

1 QUESTIONS OF IDENTITY

We now come to the first chapter of *Questioning Identity* and in it Kath Woodward starts exploring what identity actually means (Sections 1 and 2). She goes on to introduce you to some of the key social scientists who have developed the term in their work (Sections 3 and 4). Then she uses those ideas to open up and explore some case studies of uncertain and changing identities (Sections 5–8). At the same time the chapter begins to think about what constructing a social science argument involves and how we can begin to judge the kinds of knowledge and argument that social scientists generate.

KEY TASKS

Chapter 1, 'Questions of Identity'.

- Understanding what social scientists mean by identity.
- Identifying and understanding the key questions of the chapter.
- Recognizing the role of *concepts*, and *theories* in the ways social scientists construct their arguments about identity.
- Understanding DD100's model of the *circuit of knowledge*.
- Developing your writing skills.

Now please read Chapter 1, 'Questions of Identity' and return to this point in the workbook. You should spend about two thirds of your time this week on Chapter 1 and the rest on this section of the workbook.

1.1 Identity. What is it?

How did you get on with reading Chapter 1? Could you identify the main issues? Did you remember to start by asking yourself some questions? You could also have used the questions in the chapter to structure your reading.

If you think you need more help with *active reading* look back to the advice in Section 3 of the *Introductory Workbook*.

WORKBOOK ACTIVITY 1.1

As a way of checking your understanding of Chapter 1, can you pick out the main features of identity?

COMMENT

Most of the key features of identity were outlined in Sections 1 and 2 of the chapter. We listed:

- identities combine how I see myself and how others see me
- identity links the personal and the social

- identities are established by similarity and difference
- identities can be singular or multiple, fixed or fluid, individual and collective
- identities have to be adopted, we have to take up identities actively.

These features combine to produce a *concept* of identity; not just yours or mine, or ours, but what it means to talk about identity in general. What can we do with this concept? Let's try using it to address one of the framing questions posed in Chapter 1.

WORKBOOK ACTIVITY 1.2

Is there uncertainty about identity in the contemporary UK?

What evidence does the chapter offer of uncertain identities? What particular examples are used?

COMMENT

Some examples of particular uncertainties in Chapter 1 included:

Section 4 – Changes in social structures: class, gender, culture.

Section 6 – Greaves example, loss of jobs, changes in communities.

Section 7 – Kay poem, ethnic diversity, challenges to traditional ideas about being British/Scottish.

Section 8 – Body projects, new social movements, new technologies and cultural practices challenge old certainties about the limitations of the body, meanings of the body.

How can we link the general concept of identity with particular examples of uncertainties about identity? The diagram below is one take on this.

IDENTITIES LINK INDIVIDUAL TO SOCIETY
identities shaped by social structures

↓

SOCIAL STRUCTURES ARE CHANGING
i.e. class, gender, culture

↓

OLD IDENTITIES SUSTAINED BY OLD STRUCTURES ARE UNDERMINED
work, family, nation, culture

↓

NEW IDENTITIES BECOME AVAILABLE

↓

UNCERTAINTY AND DIVERSITY

Can you see how we have taken features of the general *concept* of identity, linked them together in a way that both addresses the question and draws upon the examples? Using general concepts to compare or encompass a range of individual examples is an important element of constructing a social science argument.

1.2 Constructing social science arguments

In Section 1.1 we began to construct an argument by defining a general concept of identity and applying it to a range of individual examples – it helped us to organize our material. The next stage is to generate an explanation: concepts need to be organized and animated as a *theory*.

Our starting point is Chapter 1, Section 3 where you were introduced to a range of ways in which social scientists have attempted to answer two questions about identity: 'How are identities formed?' and 'How much control do we have in the construction of our identities?'

What concepts and what theories are at work here?

WORKBOOK ACTIVITY 1.3

Look at the list of words below, they are all drawn from Section 3 of Chapter 1:

giving off information
unconscious F
imagining
roles
identification F
symbolizing
performance
sexuality F
actors

Can you note down which of these concepts is used in the work of Mead (Section 3.1), of Goffman (Section 3.2) and of Freud (Section 3.3)?

COMMENT

There is some overlap, but the concepts are mainly used as follows:

Mead: imagining, symbolizing.

Goffman: actors, roles, performance, giving off information.

Freud: identification, sexuality, unconscious.

Crudely put concepts are grouped together to produce theories and theories should generate explanations, as in the diagram:

CONCEPTS

↓

are used to create

↓

THEORIES

↓

are used to create

↓

EXPLANATIONS

We are going to use the model above to follow through the works of Mead, Goffman and Freud and to illustrate the process involved in the construction of explanations and arguments from concepts and theories.

WORKBOOK ACTIVITY 1.4

We will start with Mead. The key concepts in Chapter 1 are imagining, symbols, symbolizing and visualizing.

How can these concepts be put together to generate a theory?

COMMENT

According to Mead, in order to have an identity and to know 'who we are' we have to be able to imagine ourselves. We do this through symbols. We see pictures of ourselves in our own minds. This means that ideas, images and symbols are central to Mead's theory of identity. They are more important than the bodies we inhabit or our economic circumstances. This explanation of how identities are formed emphasizes what goes on in the heads of individuals and the use of images and symbols in the process of visualizing themselves when people decide who they are. Given this starting point what social scientists need to investigate is: what are the symbols which people use to imagine themselves?

Mead's explanation suggests that people have some degree of control over the identities which they adopt.

Let us try going through the same process with Goffman's and Freud's approaches, but this time we will represent the argument diagrammatically using the framework set out above.

Goffman on identity

CONCEPTS ↓	Roles, actors, performance, giving off information.
THEORIES ↓	Identities are acted out in everyday interactions with other people. We act out identities rather like parts in a play, where the scripts are already written, but we have some scope for giving our own version of the parts we play.
EXPLANATIONS	Identities are social, the product of the society in which we live, but people can convey information about themselves and gain information about others, about who they are, through the way people behave with each other. People are not always conscious of how they play their parts but there is some possibility of individuals interpreting their roles. We can find out about how this happens by observing everyday interaction.

Freud on identity

CONCEPTS ↓	Unconscious, identification, childhood experience, sexuality.
THEORIES ↓	Freud's psychoanalytic theory argues that identities are formed unconsciously as well as consciously; early childhood experience is important in shaping the people we become as adults; identities are fragmented and changing.
EXPLANATIONS	In order to understand identity formation in individuals we have to explore their early childhood experience and the way in which they may have repressed desires into their unconscious. It is also important to think about how individuals' gender and sexual identities are formed through childhood.

1.3 Sources of identity: writing skills

In this section we want you to try and use some of the concepts, theories and explanations developed in Chapter 1 in a short piece of writing: a mini-essay. First a few basics on essay writing in the social sciences.

1.3.1 Four golden rules of essay writing

1 Write the answer in your own words

This means that, however tempted you may be, or however much better the book you are using may seem compared with anything you could write, you have to avoid *plagiarism*. You can quote from an academic source, giving full details and using quotation marks, but you must never pass off someone else's words as your own. (See the *Introductory Workbook*, Section 8.4.) Make notes in your own words. This will help you understand the argument and use your own words when you write up an essay.

2 Answer the question asked

Spend some time thinking about what the question is actually asking. Pick out the key words and make sure you answer the question set (and not one you wish was there!).

3 Organize your material into a coherent structure

In most cases you will have to be selective. Remember the reader does not know what is on your mind so you will need to take the reader – your tutor – through the essay, making clear what you want to say and signposting each stage in the argument. For a clear structure see rule 4.

4 What a social science essay looks like

Title	Write out the title clearly, in full, at the start of the essay.
Introduction	Say what your intentions are in this essay.
Main section	Develop the key points you want to make and cite the relevant evidence to support them.
Conclusion	Sum up what you have said and make a final statement in response to the question set.
References/ bibliography	List the publications you have referred to in the essay.

We will come to more detailed guidance on social science writing in Sections 6 and 7 of this workbook. For the moment we want you to have a go using the outline above. After the title you'll probably want no more than one or two sentences for your introduction and one or two sentences for your conclusion, leaving you, in this activity, about 100 words for your main section. Make sure you include some evidence in the main section to back up your argument and *do* practise referencing your work.

WORKBOOK ACTIVITY 1.5

We would like you to choose one of the questions below and write a short piece, about 150 words (and no more), about the one you choose. The questions focus on particular aspects of identity illustrated in Chapter 1.

Question 1. In your own experience how is work linked to identity?

Here are some ideas on what you need to think about in order to answer this question.

What sort of work do you do – or did you do? Paid or unpaid? Where is/was the work done? A brief description would set the scene.

Next you need to think about the links. Go back to the definition of identity and try turning some of the features of identity into questions about the work you do. How much control do you have over your work identity? Do others define you by the work you do? Do you do this work with others? Is there a sense of belonging to a community (as in the Greaves example) where this work is done? Do you consciously share this identity with others?

How important is your work-based identity to you? Are there contradictions between this identity and other identities you have?

Question 2. What is the link between place and identity in your own life?

This could be the place where you now live or the place you come from. It could be a region or a country or a particular type of community. The Jackie Kay poem illustrates the importance of place, especially in relation to how we see ourselves and how others see us.

Do you *identify* with the place you come from or the place where you live? Is the identity associated with this place in any way distinctive or different? How do you see yourself and how are you seen by others in relation to this identity?

Question 3. How are identities represented?

This option is a bit different from the other two. Look at the Age Concern poster in Chapter 1, Section 8.1. Now pick another example of your own, for example a picture of a person from an advertisement in a magazine or newspaper. It could be the successful young professional, the street-wise teenager, the anxious mother, the good mother, the caring father. Choose one that has a clear message and which might seek to hail or interpellate a particular type of identity.

What identity is being represented? What *symbols* are used to produce meanings about this identity? Who do you think is being invited to identify with this identity and to what purpose?

There will be more opportunity to develop these skills when you get to *Study Skills Supplement 1: Reading Visual Images* and you will do more work on this with Chapter 4, but make a start here.

1.4 Social science and the circuit of knowledge

So far we have thought about the practical nuts and bolts of constructing an argument:

1 Clearly defined general *concepts* help us organize and think about particular examples of a phenomenon.

2 *Concepts* can be combined together to generate *theories* which are general frameworks for providing explanations of phenomena.

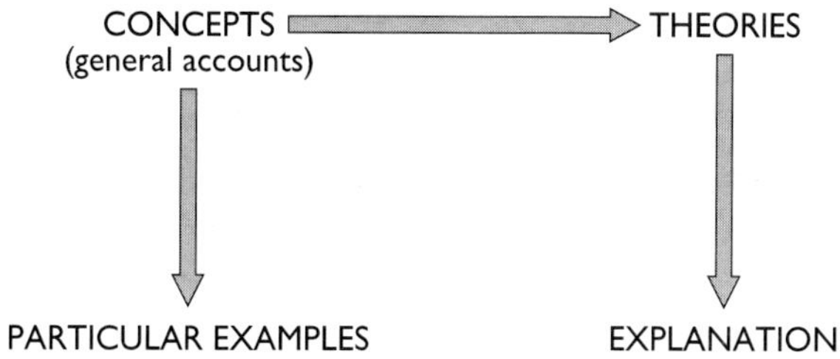

But how do we begin to examine and evaluate the quality of those concepts, theories and explanations?

You may recall from our discussion of the progress of the argument in the *Introductory Chapter* (see Sections 2–4) that:

- Social science enquiry starts with questions.
- Evaluating answers to these questions requires us to sharpen up our argument. We need to generate specific claims, descriptive or explanatory, that are fit for rigorous exploration.
- Social scientists reach for evidence when examining these kinds of claims.
- Evidence does not speak for itself – but must be carefully handled, sifted and interpreted.
- This process is broadly what we call *evaluation* – a process which often generates new questions to be resolved as well as confirming or contradicting the original claims.

In DD100 we have linked these processes of enquiry together in what we call the *circuit of knowledge*, see Figure 3(a).

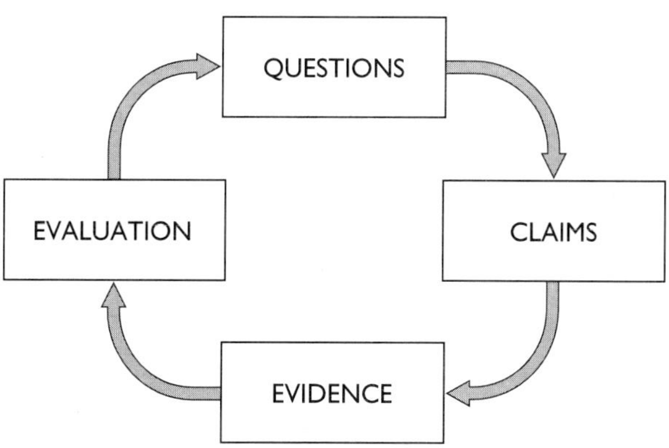

FIGURE 3(a) The circuit of knowledge I

You will find later in DD100 how concepts, theories and the arguments one can construct out of them also shape the way we use evidence and do our evaluation. But for the moment just think about concepts and theories as a way of generating descriptive and explanatory claims, see Figure 3(b).

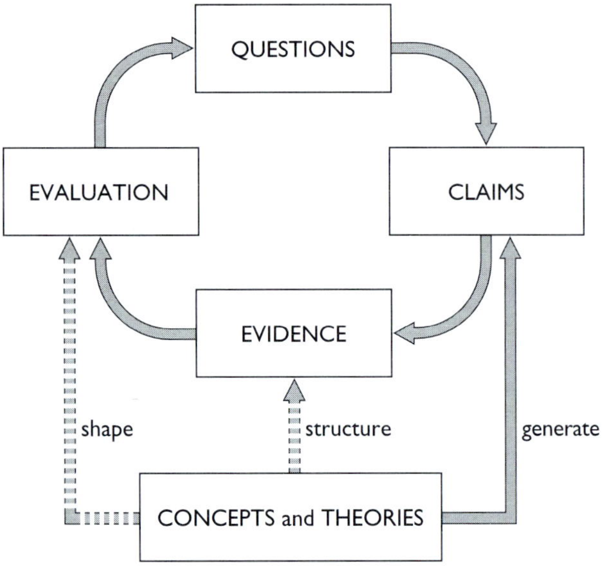

FIGURE 3(b) The circuit of knowledge II

Let us see how it works in a bit more detail in Chapter 1.

Questions

Chapter 1 began with three framing questions.

How are identities formed?

How much control do we have in shaping our own identities?

Are there particular uncertainties about identity in the contemporary UK?

In order to begin answering these big questions the chapter tries to focus on more specific manageable claims. Kath Woodward picks out areas of identity which might be particularly important. We will focus on issues of work and work-based identities.

So we can rephrase our questions as:

How are work-based identities formed?

How much control do we have over work-based identities?

Are there uncertainties about work-based identities in the contemporary UK?

But what claims does Chapter 1 make in response to these questions and how do concepts and theories of identities developed in Chapter 1 help us generate those claims?

Claims

Drawing specifically on the arguments of Mead, Goffman and the accounts of social structures in Section 4 of Chapter 1, we picked out these claims.

- Work-based identities are formed by the interaction of individuals with economic structures which generate a repertoire of roles, symbols and conventions that individuals take up and identify with.
- Individual control over work-based identities are structured, patterned and constrained by the pre-existing conditions of work and distribution of economic opportunity.
- Individuals may have more choice over whether they choose to identify with work-based identities than other identities such as gender or place.
- For men who have worked in traditional industrial sectors, work-based identities have become more uncertain.

Evidence

The next step Kath Woodward takes is to look for some information against which these kinds of claims can be tested.

John Greaves's autobiographical account offers one type of evidence about the importance of work and identity. This piece suggests that structural changes in the economy can have significant impacts upon identities.

WORKBOOK ACTIVITY 1.6

Look back at your notes on Section 6.

1. **What does John Greaves's writing tell us about how identities are formed?**
2. **How much control did he have in shaping his work-based identity?**
3. **Does his account suggest that there is greater uncertainty about work identities in the late 1990s?**

COMMENT

1. John's account suggests that paid work, especially in work like coal mining, is a very important dimension of identity. Miners lived in a community dominated socially and economically by the coal industry. There is a strong connection between personal experience and the social factors related to paid work, and a strong sense of belonging – of being the same as others within the community.
2. Within coal mining communities there was little room for the expression of alternative identities to work-based ones – for men at any rate, so all-encompassing was the place of coal mining in the life of the community. External social forces that brought about the collapse of the mining industry clearly had, and still have, significant impact on the identity of John and those who live in his community.
3. This account does suggest there are greater uncertainties about identity, especially work-based identities in the coal industry (and other heavy manufacturing industries) in the UK. This is illustrated by the irony of the old Coal Board slogan 'A Job for Life'. For many people like John, who had expected that to be the case, they were left not only without a particular job, but without any job, in a community which had been prosperous and was, by the late 1990s, impoverished.

The activity above begins to explore the relationships between asking questions and making claims and using evidence. However, you are probably already thinking of some more questions which we could be asking about our example of the link between work and identity. In particular, one person's account might not be representative of the UK as a whole, or even coal miners in general. We need more *quantitative* evidence; especially to address the question about greater uncertainty in relation to changing social structures.

The evidence we have looked at so far is qualitative and provides significant insights into the personal side of the identity equation. It takes on board personal feelings as well as conveying the sense of community at two different moments in time, but it would be useful to know more about the scale of pit closures and of alternative employment which might have become available, for example. Is this story only about men? The community John describes is one peopled by women, men and children. What might be missing from this account?

Evaluation

How far have we gone around the circuit of knowledge? We started by focusing our general framing questions into more specific work-identity related questions. We drew on theories of identity to generate specific, sharper claims and looked at one piece of autobiographical evidence.

However, as we evaluate the original claim, in the light of evidence available to us, we might need to consider some more questions. What else do we need to know? What would more quantitative evidence about economic change and employment add? John Greaves's story is an account of a changing work-based identity but it is also a gendered account. It would also be interesting and useful to find out about the experiences of women in the community and whether a changing work identity had an impact on gender identity too. By comparing the work, paid and unpaid, and home experiences of women and men we might come up with a different set of claims about identity. We started with questions and the investigation has led to the addition of more questions as we complete our circuit of knowledge (see Figure 4). This leads us to Chapter 2, which asks more questions about gender and gendered identities.

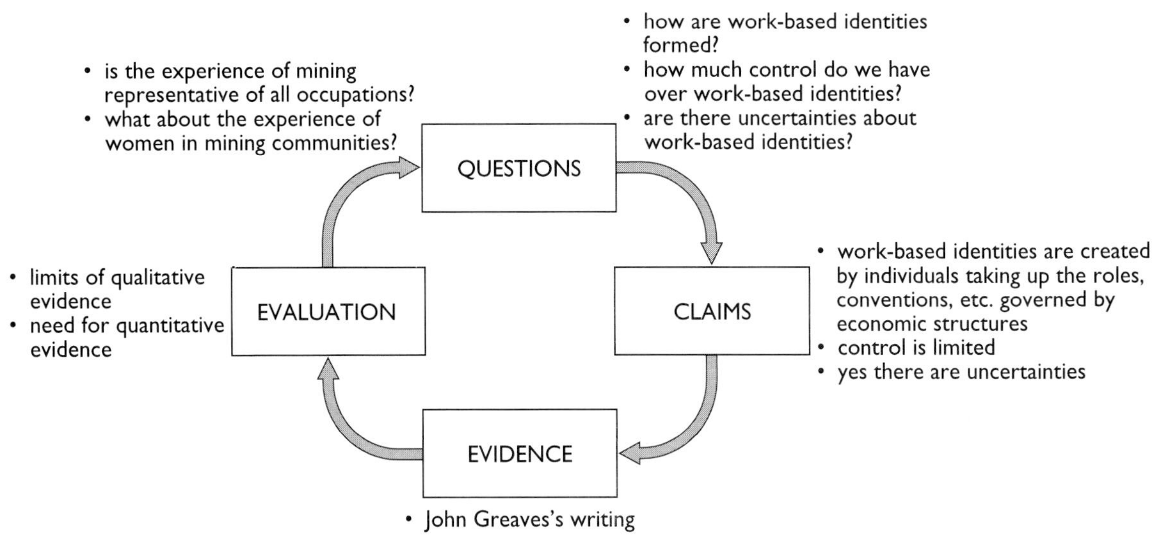

FIGURE 4 The circuit of knowledge with comments based on our work on Chapter 1

2 IDENTITY AND GENDER

In Chapter 1 you looked at three sources of identity: the work we do, the places we come from, and our bodies and biology. Each of these sources of identity offered both the promise of certainty in a changing world and causes of new uncertainties and contradictions.

The three chapters that follow each focus on just one of these sources of identity. In Chapter 2 we look at how far our identities could be shaped by our biology and ask: by what mechanisms and processes might our genes or our bodies determine who we are? Whether we are male or female, old or young, able bodied or disabled, what kind of social consequences flow from these embodied origins?

The authors of Chapter 2, Jenny Gove and Stuart Watt, begin by thinking about how biological and social structures are entwined in shaping gender identities (Sections 1 and 2). They go on to explore how children learn to recognize gender identities (Section 3) and take on gender identities themselves. They then take just one of many current issues to illustrate these debates: the differences in educational achievement between boys and girls (Section 4). This provides an opportunity to unpack how a social science argument is constructed. In working through these arguments, they will also look in more detail at the types of evidence social scientists draw upon, and some of the skills required for working with numbers and gathering evidence in the social sciences.

KEY TASKS

Chapter 2, 'Identity and Gender'.

- Understanding some social science accounts of gender identity and its entwined biological and social origins.
- Understanding what psychologists mean by stereotypes, categorization and cognitive development, and how they use these concepts to explain identity formation.
- Recognizing some of the methods of research used by psychologists.
- Reading simple arithmetical material relating to educational achievement and describing the patterns it shows.
- Being able to take a social science argument and show how it has been constructed. (In this case one relating to educational achievement and identity.)

Please read Chapter 2, 'Identity and Gender' and return to this point in the workbook.

For this study week you should spend around two thirds of your time reading the chapter and the rest on this section of the workbook.

2.1 Chapter 2. What's it about?

WORKBOOK ACTIVITY 2.1

In order to check your understanding of the chapter we would like you to think how Chapter 2 addresses one of the framing questions of the book about identity formation. Look back at your notes and think about this question:

How are identities formed? In particular, what does Chapter 2 tell us about how gendered identities are formed?

Try organizing your response into a diagram which covers some of the different concepts and theories which the chapter offers.

COMMENT

We picked out the following concepts as important to the production of the key arguments in Chapter 2.

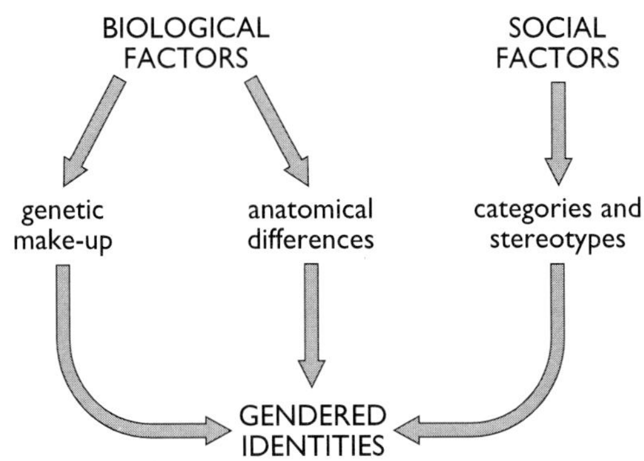

As we know, the gendered identities that we possess are women/female or man/male. These categories are conceptualized differently by different social scientists and others. Some see them as fixed, essentialist categories. Others see more 'grey area' and think of them as fuzzy or non-essentialist categories.

Section 3 of the chapter makes clear that the ways in which we define and use these categories is developed in childhood, but then changes as children seem to recognize, at first, simple anatomical gendered categories and then learn to recognize more complex social categories.

We can represent the account of the formation of gendered identities in Chapter 2 diagrammatically.

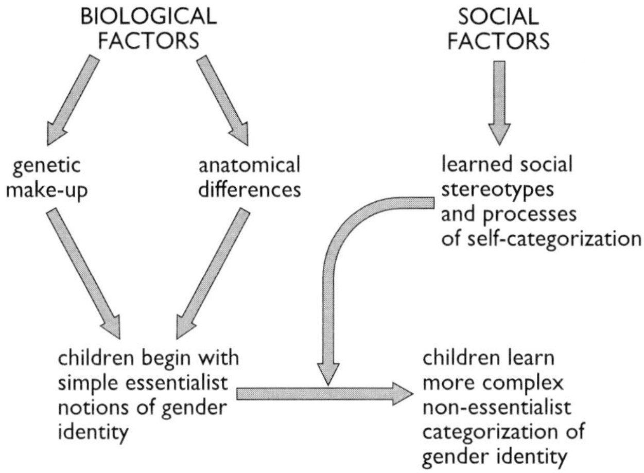

2.1.1 More about evidence

Chapter 2 draws on a range of different types of evidence: social and biological evidence used to allocate people to gender categories in Section 1, transcripts of children's conversations and accounts of role play in Section 3, and quantitative statistical evidence of educational performance in Section 4.

The type of evidence used by social scientists varies, as do the *methods* which they employ to obtain that evidence. For example, in Section 3, in studying the development of young children, psychologists have used direct *observational* methods, while Section 4 draws upon indirect statistical methods. The methods employed are influenced by the kind of evidence which social scientists seek to obtain, for example, whether that evidence is qualitative or quantitative.

In the next section we are going to look in more detail at using quantitative data as evidence. You might feel comfortable with such material, in which case you can skip Section 2.2, but if you feel anxious about dealing with numbers work through the material below.

2.2 Gender differences in educational achievement: working with numbers

The first half of Chapter 2 focused on how we construct gender categories and how children learn to use these categories. Now we come to the question of how far these gendered identities influence childrens' behaviour in schools and, specifically, their achievement in examinations. Until recently the dominant political concerns in this field were about girls' under-achievement in school. Recently the issue of boys' under-achievement has hit the headlines and boys' GCSE results have helped trigger these concerns.

Figure 2.5 of Chapter 2 is a bar chart which shows the GCSE results of girls and boys in different subjects. Bar charts are a very useful way to display information, so let's pause here a moment and work through the skills involved in reading this one. (Part of Figure 2.5 is reproduced in Section 2.2.2 below.)

The figure is a bar chart showing results in percentages so there are two skills involved. One is understanding percentages, the other is reading bar charts displaying them. Let us start with percentages.

2.2.1 Percentages

Percentages are a very common and useful way to describe exact parts of something. The most common way to describe a part of something is to use forms like 'a half' or 'a quarter', but when you want to describe a part which is not a half, a quarter or a third, or you want to be very precise, then percentages are very convenient. They are used frequently in newspapers – and in social science courses.

This section of the workbook aims to ensure you really understand this useful idea. If you are sure you do, just do the exercises to check, but for many people percentages are a bit of a mystery; so here is a short introduction.

You recognize a percentage by the symbol %. It is read as 'per cent' and it means 'out of a hundred'. So, if out of 100 children in a room, 5 are girls and 95 are boys you can say that 5% of those in the room are girls and 95% are boys.

Things are not quite so straightforward if there are fewer or more than 100 children in the room. Then, in order to work out the percentages of girls and boys, we need to do some calculations. The calculations are worth doing because in the social sciences they offer an easy way to *compare* proportions when you need to do so. Let us see how this works.

WORKBOOK ACTIVITY 2.2

Suppose there are only 50 children in the room. 5 of them are girls and 45 are boys.

What percentage of the children are girls? Try to work it out for yourself first. If you do not know how, just read on.

COMMENT

10% of the children are girls. Here are a couple of ways of working that answer out. See which is clearer to you.

Out of 50 children, 5 are girls. To calculate the girls as a percentage of the total, we have to treat the whole group of 50 as if they were 100. We need to multiply by 2 to turn 50 into 100. Then we multiply the number of girls by 2 as well. 5 out of 50 is the same as 10 out of 100 or 10%.

Alternatively, we can state the proportion of girls as

$$\frac{5}{50}$$

Then to turn the fraction into a percentage, you just multiply by 100

$$\frac{5}{50} \times 100$$

You can work out the answer to that by hand or on a calculator. We advise a calculator! On a calculator, you first divide 5 by 50, then multiply the answer by 100. Try it now, and check that you get the answer 10.

By hand, you need to 'cancel' the fraction like this: first divide top and bottom of the first fraction by 5

$$\frac{5 \quad \text{divide by } 5}{50 \quad \text{divide by } 5} = \frac{1}{10}$$

then multiply the result by 100

$$\frac{1}{10} \times 100 = \frac{100}{10} = 10$$

You do not need to understand that calculation to work happily with percentages. The calculator method is just fine.

We can now turn that calculation into a rule:

> **Rule 1: Calculating a percentage.** To express one number as a percentage of another, divide the first number by the second and multiply by 100.

WORKBOOK ACTIVITY 2.3

Check your understanding of this rule by using a calculator to answer the following:

1 You get 42 marks out of 70 for an assignment. What is your mark as a percentage?

2 In an (imaginary) UK opinion poll in 1999, 2,500 people were asked who Gordon Brown was. 425 did not know. What percentage had never heard of the Chancellor of the Exchequer?

3 In a group of 325 people, 65 own a computer and 52 have access to one at work. Express that statement in percentages.

C O M M E N T

1 60%

2 17%

3 20% own a computer and 16% have access to one at work.

2.2.2 Reading bar charts

Now let us return to the bar chart and have a careful look at this way of displaying information. Bar charts are really good at showing quantitative data in ways which allow the reader to absorb and understand them. They are worth a bit of effort to get used to them. We are not going to worry here about drawing them, just reading them.

Reproduced here as Figure 5 are just two parts of Figure 2.5 from Chapter 2: the results for English and Maths, for girls and for boys. Start by reading the title: it says these are results for 16-year-olds showing the percentage of girls and the percentage of boys achieving GCSE results A*–C.

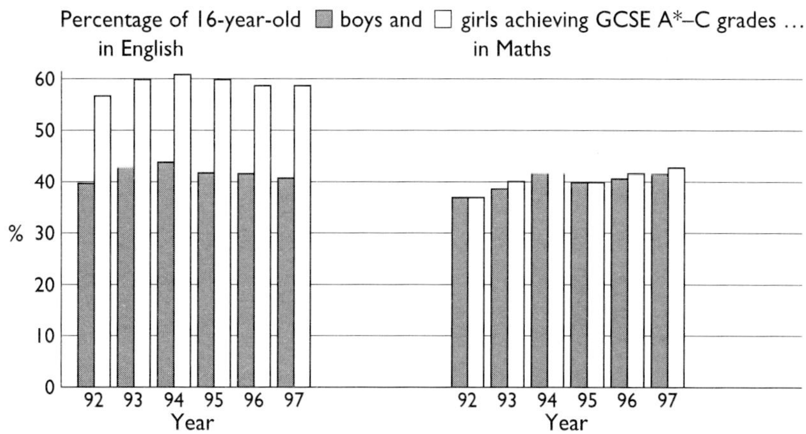

FIGURE 5 Bar chart of girls' and boys' GCSE results

Source: *The Observer*, 4 January 1998

Now look at the *axes*, that is, the horizontal line across the bottom and the vertical line up the left-hand side. Read the labels on these axes carefully. The vertical one shows the percentages defined in the title, from 0 up to 60%. The horizontal axis reads '92', '93' ... '97', so this shows a series of years. The chart is going to show percentages for each year, so we can look at changes over time. Finally there is a *key* or *legend*: this tells us which of the bars for each year refers to girls, and which to boys.

WORKBOOK ACTIVITY 2.4

Look first at the English GCSE part of the bar chart. Explain in words what it shows, without looking back at the chapter.

COMMENT

It shows that girls have consistently done better than boys, and that this has not changed a great deal. Around 60% of girls achieved A*–C grades each year from 1993 to 1997, and a slightly lower percentage in 1992. Only about 40% of boys managed the same grades in 1992 and from 1995 to 1997, and somewhat more than 40% in 1993 and 1994. There is no trend: that is, the percentages are not consistently rising or falling over the six years.

WORKBOOK ACTIVITY 2.5

Now Maths: what does it show, and how does it compare with English?

COMMENT

In Maths, the performance of boys and girls is very similar. And there is a trend: results have been getting somewhat better over the six years. Comparing Maths and English, we see that boys produce very similar results in the two subjects – hovering around 40% obtaining A*–C grades in both. However, a higher percentage of girls do well in English than in Maths.

2.3 Murphy and Elwood: constructing a social science argument

Having identified some key differences in boys' and girls' GCSE results, Jenny Gove and Stuart Watt take you through a range of possible explanations. They look at biological and cognitive factors and a range of social factors. They focus on the arguments of Murphy and Elwood: that childrens' gendered identities lead them, in general, to tackle school-work differently and to perform differently in exams. I now want you to use their account of Murphy and Elwood's argument to help you think further about how social science arguments are constructed.

Chapter 2 shows that three claims form the core of Murphy and Elwood's work.

- *Claim 1:* Boys and girls foster different interests, attitudes, and behaviours prior to attending school, which are then perpetuated within school.

- *Claim 2:* Feminine and masculine identities are perceived in particular ways by teachers, with consequences that may impinge on achievement.
- *Claim 3:* In their school-work, girls and boys draw upon the different interests and skills that they have developed through their gendered experiences.

How are these claims put together? How is the argument constructed?

Look back at your notes and think about what is involved in the first claim.

Claim 1

This claim draws upon the biological, cognitive and social arguments which were introduced in Section 2. The interaction between these different components in early childhood development are seen as maintained in the school context. What constitutes typically gendered behaviour draws upon stereotypical gendered characteristics.

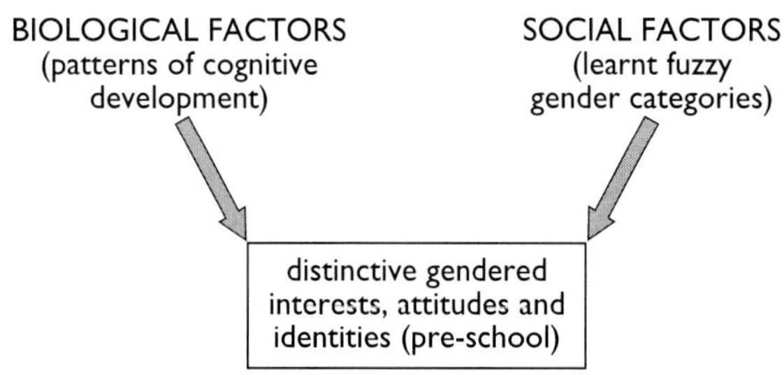

Claim 2

This claim argues that those pre-school attitudes and identities are reinforced by teachers, and lead to distinct gendered patterns of behaviour in skills with direct consequences for school performance and achievement.

Claim 3

This claim focuses on the cognitive skills which girls and boys have developed through their early childhood development. These skills directly impact on performance, though in different ways in different subjects.

The three claims combine to produce an argument which seeks to explain gendered behaviour and differential educational achievement in terms of an interaction between individual girls and boys and the social world which they inhabit. Typical gendered attitudes and attributes are reinforced and rewarded in the school setting so that children and young people develop and reinforce particular skills. Cognitive skills are developed and reinforced through social and educational experience. What is typical draws on gendered categories as discussed in Section 2. There is scope for reconstruction of categories here, and not everyone conforms, but the process, as the two diagrams show, is cumulative. It builds up to add extra factors and shows how gender identities are reinforced through an interaction between different factors, biological and social.

So we can represent the structure of the argument as a whole diagrammatically.

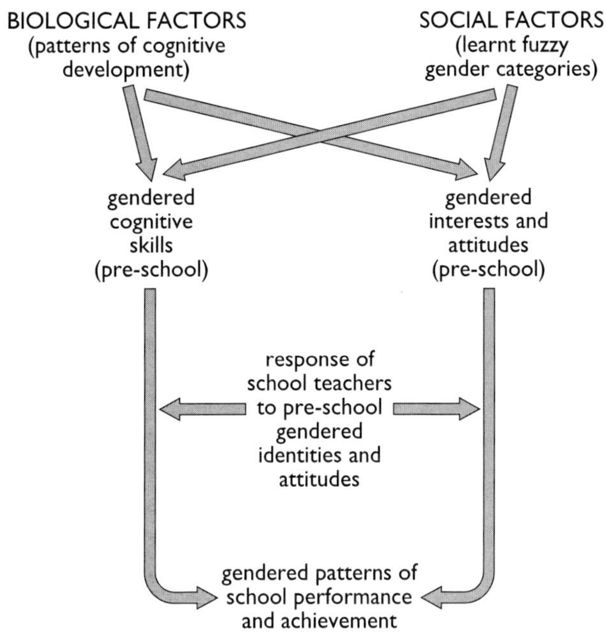

3 IDENTITY, INEQUALITY AND SOCIAL CLASS

We started in Chapter 1 with an overview of the question of identity, its multiple forms and origins. In Chapter 2 we focused on biology as a source of identity and used gender as a way of exploring this. In Chapter 3 we are going to consider a second source of identity: material and economic circumstances and look at class as a way of exploring this relationship. How important as a source of identity are our incomes, the jobs we have, the class we belong to, or what we spend our money on? Is class, in particular, still of key importance in deciding who we are and how others see us? Have the certainties once associated with class disintegrated and if so what, if anything, is replacing them? Engaging with these questions will require you to build on some of the skills you have already practised – using numbers, interpreting meanings and constructing arguments.

KEY TASKS

Chapter 3, 'Identity, Inequality and Social Class'.

- Understanding the kinds of questions social scientists ask about poverty, income and class, and their relationship to identity.
- Understanding how these questions can address the course themes of *uncertainty and diversity* and *structure and agency*.
- Using numerical data to describe income inequalities in the UK today and the way these inequalities are changing.
- Acquiring an understanding of the writings of Marx and Weber on class divisions and identities in society and being able to compare the ideas of Marx and Weber.
- Acquiring an understanding of the role of economic consumption in forming identities.
- Working further around the circuit of knowledge looking at the assessment and evaluation of claims and the role of comparison as part of this process.

▶ Now please read Chapter 3 and then return to this part of the workbook. You should spend about two-thirds of your time working on Chapter 3 and the remaining time on this section of the workbook.

3.1 Getting orientated: economics and identity

When you finish working through a chapter it is worth seeing whether you can quickly draw together the strands of its argument. If nothing else it should help make clear to you the links or the arguments you are unsure about and identify areas that will need more work as you go through the workbook.

WORKBOOK ACTIVITY 3.1

Skim through your notes on Sections 1, 3 and 4: how could you diagrammatically represent the relationship of the key concepts and links in the chapter, above all the relationships between economic structures and identities?

COMMENT

There are lots of ways of doing this. We took the argument of Section 1 as the core of the chapter.

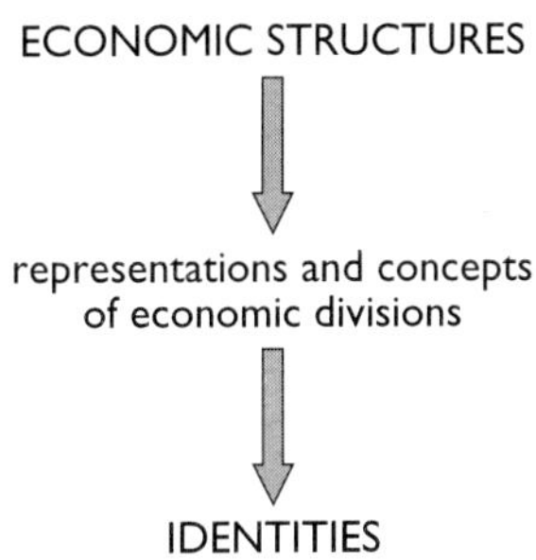

But what economic structures? Section 3 emphasizes the importance of paid work – the jobs we do, and Section 4 emphasizes the importance of financial wealth. Paid work and financial wealth are unequally distributed and generate inequalities in income (Section 3) and power (Section 4). So we could expand our diagram like this.

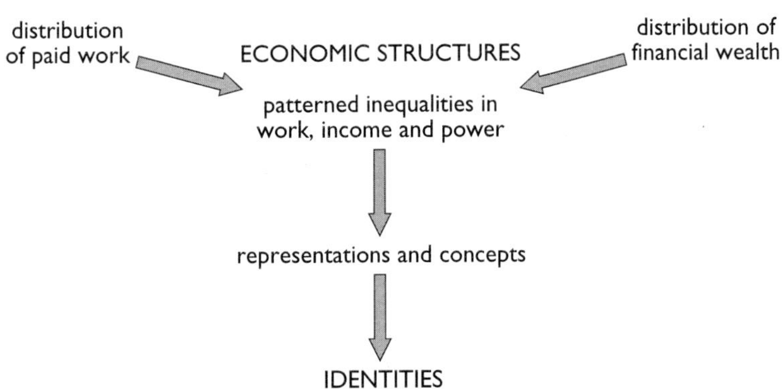

Chapter 3 looks at a number of different ways in which social scientists and the public in general represent or conceptualize those patterned inequalities. Sections 2 and 4 look at notions of poverty and wealth, Section 5 looks at Marx's and Weber's theories of class and changes in the structure of work. Section 6 looks at two accounts of the role of economic consumption in determining identity in the work of the sociologists Peter Saunders and Pierre Bourdieu and Section 7 looks at changes in patterned inequalities of income and power (social polarization) and a new attempt to represent and conceptualize its consequences for identities (social exclusion).

The key debates within this field are:

- which model of class best copes with changes in the structure of work?
- have class identities, as economic structures change, become less central and certain; what other economic identities, if any, are replacing them?

WORKBOOK ACTIVITY 3.2

How could you graft the points above, and any others you think are central to the chapter, on to the diagram?

COMMENT

We tried this.

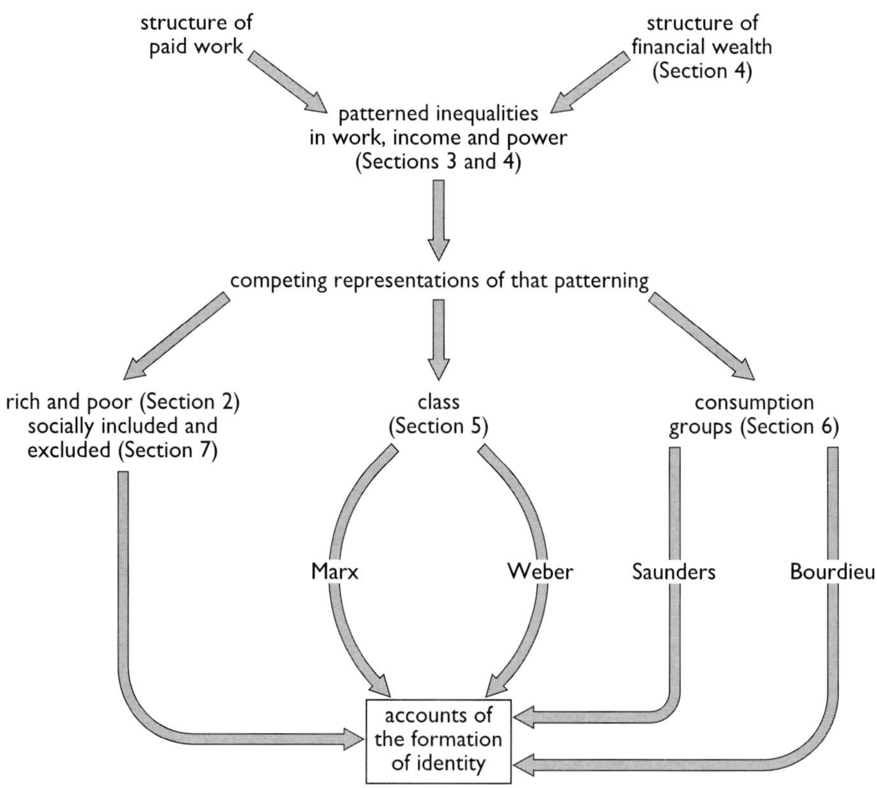

We're going to look at economic change, class and consumption identities in more detail later. Why do the authors of Chapter 3 focus on these? Why do the concepts of the 'poor' and 'socially excluded' not translate into economic identities?

WORKBOOK ACTIVITY 3.3

Being poor is something we might expect to have important implications for the way a person sees himself or herself; to be a clear source of identity. As Section 2 makes clear this is not the case. Why not?

Do the *socially excluded* posses a culture and identity that are different from the mainstream?

Jot down some notes now from your reading of Sections 2 and 7.

COMMENT

We noted:

- There is disagreement over what we mean by poverty and how we define it. Poverty means different things to different people. Politicians and those on low incomes disagree over the meaning of poverty.
- Poverty is relative. What you need depends on what others have and what others expect.
- Poverty is seen to carry a stigma and, as the last paragraph in Section 2 makes clear, many of those who might be categorized as poor do not see themselves in this way at all. Being poor is a label which can be resisted or challenged or rejected.
- Jordan's research, quoted in Section 7, suggests that the socially excluded have values and aspirations which are very similar to the rest of society.

The core issues which the rest of this section of the workbook focuses on can be represented diagrammatically.

①

②

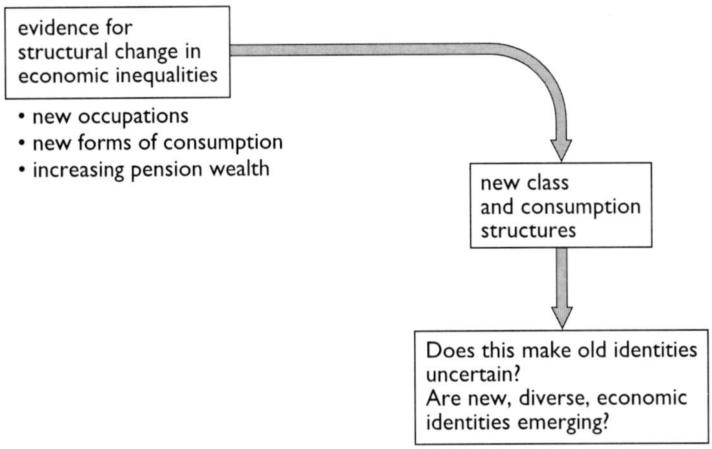

In Section 3.2 we go on to focus on the skills you need to tackle debates on patterned inequalities in income and wealth. In Section 3.3 we work through the debates about class and the relationship between class structures and identities. In Section 3.4 we will tackle the issues of uncertainty and diversity in economic identity.

3.2 How unequal are we? Using numerical data

In Chapter 3, Section 3 you were introduced to the income parade. Engaging with this image of the income distribution required you to draw on the skills you developed in your study of Chapter 2 (see Section 2.2 of this workbook). In addition, Chapter 3 asked you to think more about how to compare percentages and to think about averages. This part of the workbook offers more help with these skills. Once again, those of you who are confident of your numerical skills should skim this section and move on to Section 3.3.

3.2.1 Comparing percentages

One of the most useful things about percentages is that it allows you to *compare* proportions of *differently* sized populations. Let's make sure you understand just how such comparisons work.

Suppose in one local authority area the population is 300,000 people. Of these, 39,000 define themselves as black, 27,000 refuse to classify themselves, and the rest classify themselves as white.

In a second area, the population is 550,000. 60,500 classify themselves as black, 49,500 refuse to classify themselves, and the rest call themselves white.

WORKBOOK ACTIVITY 3.4

Which area has the higher percentage of people classifying themselves as white and as black? Which area has the higher percentage refusing to answer the question?

COMMENT

Area 1. By self-classification the population is 13% black, 78% white, and 9% refuse to answer.

Area 2. On the same basis, the population is 11% black, 80% white, with 9% refusing to answer.

So the first area has a higher percentage of black people, the second a higher percentage of white people, and the percentage of refusals is the same in both areas.

3.2.2 Averages

Chapter 3, Section 3 uses the idea of average household incomes. Are you happy with the idea of an average? This exercise helps you to check.

WORKBOOK ACTIVITY 3.5

Three households, all containing two adults, one child and an elderly person, have the following annual incomes: £9,700, £11,400, £35,000. What is the average household income?

COMMENT

To answer the question, add up the incomes and divide by 3. The total of the three incomes in £56,100. Dividing by 3 gives an average household income of £18,700.

A second rule of thumb then is:

> **Rule 2: Calculating averages.** To calculate the average of a list of numbers, first add up the numbers and write down the total. Then count the numbers in the list, and divide the total by the count.

Look back at the example of household incomes above. The *average* income is well above the middle income of the three. This is because there is a big gap between the first two incomes and the third. So when you average them, the top income pulls the average up above the other two incomes. This is the effect we saw in real life in the UK income parade in Chapter 3. Income distributions tend to look like this. There are usually a relatively small number of very wealthy people, and their incomes pull *average* incomes up above the income of the household half-way along the parade. The income of the household half-way along is called by statisticians the *median* income.

3.3 Understanding social class

At the core of Chapter 3 are two theories of class – theories with distinct sets of descriptive and explanatory claims which allow us to bridge the gap between patterned inequalities of work/income and identities. In this section of the workbook we are going to re-examine these theories and begin to evaluate and compare them.

WORKBOOK ACTIVITY 3.6

You will be doing a substantial amount of work on comparing theories later in the course (particularly in Blocks 4 and 5) so this is really just a first try at something which will become quite familiar to you. The grid below gives you the opportunity to think about the similarities and differences between Marxist and Weberian approaches to class.

Fill in the empty boxes as far as you are able. These are some of the core claims of the theories. Then look at the completed grid at the back of this workbook (p.69) to help with those boxes you found difficult.

Marx and Weber

	Marx	Weber
What is the structural basis of class divisions?		
Is class the main division in society?		
How many classes are there in capitalist societies?		
What relationship exists between classes?		
How and under what conditions do class divisions generate identities?		

How can we begin to compare these two accounts of class? Which makes more sense of the relationships between economic structures and identities? Making that judgement takes us back to the circuit of knowledge.

What is the key question being addressed here?

One way of putting it would be: How well do Marx's and Weber's theories of class explain how economic structures generate class identities?

Now we need to sharpen up this question into examinable claims for both Marx's theory and Weber's theory. How would you condense their arguments into a claim? We came up with:

Marx	Unequal and exploitative structures of capital ownership define economic classes. That inequality generates class conflict and class-consciousness and the embedding of class identities.
Weber	Unequal and parallel inequalities in access to and power in the labour market define economic classes.
	Economic competition between classes generates loose class identities.
	Social status and collective organization both within and outside the economic realm create more entrenched identities.

The next step, as you will now know, is to search out some evidence. Look back at the call centre case study and Chapter 3, Activity 3.3 (Section 5.4) for an example of this.

The comment on Activity 3.3 of Chapter 3 begins the final stage of the circuit of knowledge: evaluating the two sets of claims in the light of the evidence and pointing towards some new questions that might be asked.

3.4 The decline of old certainties: the construction of an argument

The call centre case study illustrates the issues of uncertainty and diversity. Changing economic structures and technologies may be re-creating and re-inventing class divisions, or they may, in some circumstances, be undermining old identities and generating new ones in their place. This is stated explicitly in Section 6.

Once again let's see if we can organize these arguments diagrammatically.

WORKBOOK ACTIVITY 3.7

Section 6 tackles the issue of uncertainty and class identities from a number of angles. How can we represent them diagrammatically?

Have a go yourself.

If you are not sure where to start, try to construct your notes around the following questions:

- What are the core elements of the concept of class?
- What do we mean by the old certainties of class?
- What are the two ways in which it is argued they are being eroded?
- What evidence is cited of a move from collective to individualist identities?
- What are the two theories which argue that class identities have been displaced or transformed by divisions based on consumption?
- How can you sum up what the section is saying about the erosion of certainties?

COMMENT

We came up with the following.

We noted that class identities share two elements:

1 They are collective identities.

2 They are identities rooted in occupations (both Marxist and Weberian models).

So:

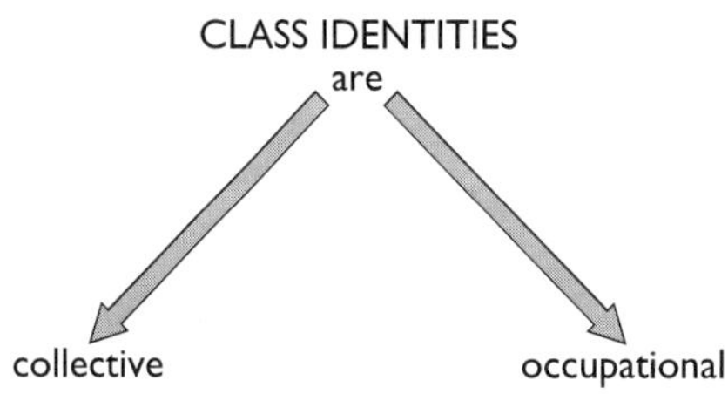

Section 6 identifies three social science arguments that believe these identities are eroding:

Goldthorpe *et al.* on Luton car workers

Saunders on consumption cleavages

Bourdieu on social significance of consumption.

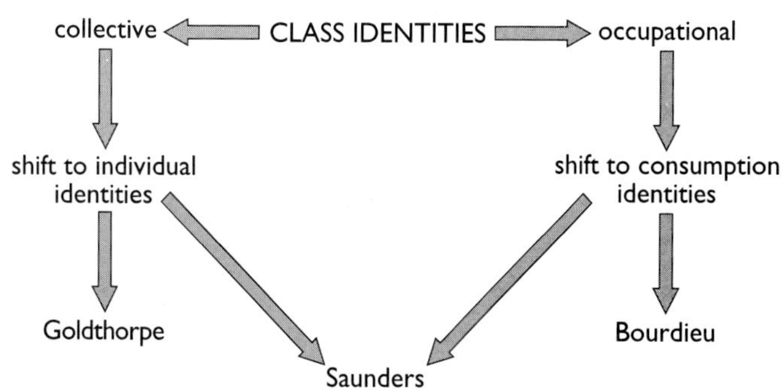

As well as clarifying your notes this kind of exercise takes you one step further in your understanding of how arguments are constructed. In Chapter 2 we looked at the argument presented by Murphy and Elwood to explain patterns of educational achievement. We saw how it could be broken down into a number of linked claims each supported by examples and evidence and each linked to the previous one in a clearly signposted way. In this case what we are working on is more complex. We have a number of separate arguments, all converging to make the same general point, that class identity is becoming less certain. The construction of each argument internally is exactly the same as for the Murphy and Elwood example, i.e. it consists of a number of general statements supported by examples and evidence all linked to each other and building on each other. Each of these arguments is now linked to other statements to present a larger, more complex and comprehensive argument.

WORKBOOK ACTIVITY 3.8

What accounts for these shifts? What helps explain the erosion of old class identities for each of these arguments? What evidence is presented in Section 6 in support of these arguments? How could you graft this on to the above diagram?

COMMENT

We completed our diagram like this.

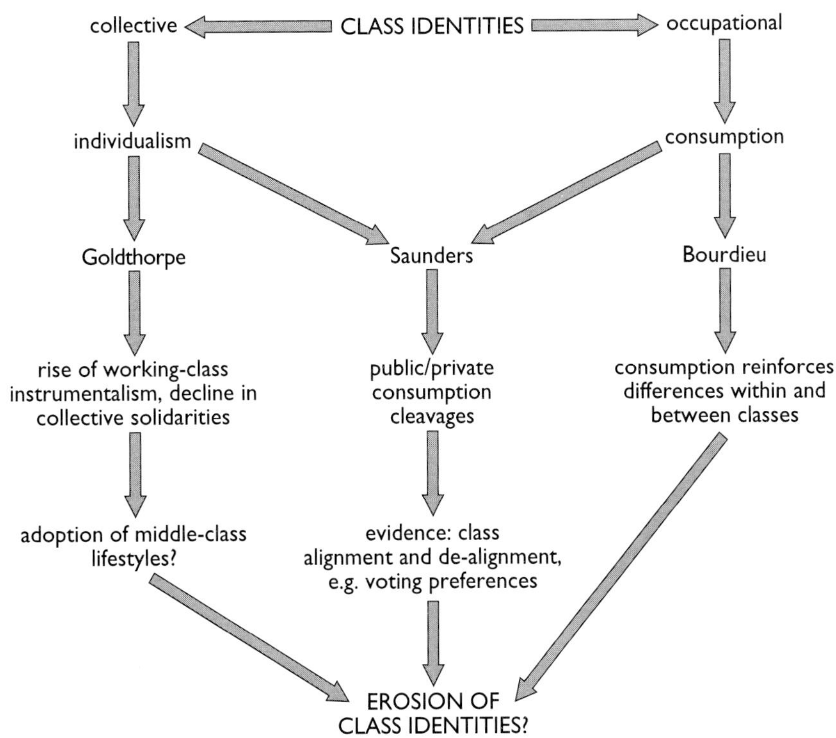

So has the significance and certainties of class identities in the UK diminished? On balance Chapter 3 has delivered claims, arguments and evidence that point in both directions. Marxist accounts of call centres suggest class identities change but endure; accounts of the death of class may have been exaggerated. Weberian theories suggest that class identities may endure, but become more uncertain as they are criss-crossed by diverse alternative hierarchies and identities. Consumption may be one of these hierarchies, but as Bourdieu notes this may reinforce class differences and identities rather than extinguishing them.

Evaluation, as you can see, is a complex process of sifting evidence, examining the case for and against and generating new questions. For a more definitive answer we would want to look at more areas of work than call centres, gather more data on consumption and identity, and ask more questions of more people about their identities.

▶ Now read *Study Skills Supplement 1: Reading Visual Images* and listen to the associated audio-cassette (Audio-cassette 2). Then return to this point in the workbook.

4 IDENTITY AND NATION

Chapter 4 explores a third possible source of identity alongside class and gender: the place we come from. You touched on this in Chapter 1. Chapter 4 takes this a lot further, using the nation you belong to as an example of place. The main questions of the chapter are concerned with British identity and whether 'being British' is an increasingly uncertain source of identity. Exploring these issues will require you to draw on some of the concepts used by political scientists: *nations*, *states* and *nation-states*. Other concepts will be more familiar: *meanings*, *interpretations* and *culture* in the construction of identities. In addition, you will also need some historical background to be able to understand the character and complexity of national identities. As you work through Chapter 4 and the workbook we will be returning to the role of concepts and theories in constructing social science arguments, in this case about the formation of national identities, and the role of reading visual images in the social sciences.

KEY TASKS

Chapter 4, 'Identity and Nation'.

- Understanding the origins and character of national identity and the role of concepts and theories in doing so.
- Understanding what is meant in this chapter by culture and exploring how national identities are constructed through culture.
- Exploring the course themes of *uncertainty and diversity*, and *structure and agency* in relation to national identity.
- Being able to read visual images, including maps, and relate these to debates about national identity.
- Constructing an argument for yourself based on the central questions of the chapter.

Now please read Chapter 4, 'Identity and Nation' and return to this point in the workbook. You should spend around two-thirds of your time on Chapter 4 and the remainder with this section of the workbook.

4.1 Where do you come from? Place, culture and identity

The starting point for this chapter is the way our identities are constructed in relation to place, but you have been here already!

WORKBOOK ACTIVITY 4.1

In Chapter 1, Section 7, Kath Woodward used the poem *So You Think I'm a Mule* by Jackie Kay to explore some of the relationships between *place* and identity. (You might find it useful at this point to look back at the relevant section of Chapter 1.)

The extracts from Tony Parker's work which open Chapter 4 also allow us to make a number of significant points about this relationship. Below I have noted three of the key points which Kath made in her commentary on the Kay poem. Try for yourself to note down how and to what extent similar points emerge from the Belfast material.

1. The poem is a comment on the need of the white woman to locate Kay and her response to the uncertainty which Kay presents.
2. Locating Kay is so important to the white woman because she sees the world in terms of us and them, the pure white and the other.
3. Her disquiet is due to the way in which the clues we use to locate people (accent, appearance, birth place) can give off contradictory messages.

COMMENT

1. What runs through the Parker extract, as it does through the poem, is the need for certainty; the need to locate or define people in some way. In the case of Belfast to define someone as being Protestant or Catholic. Parker suggests that 'no relationship can proceed unless certain basics are clarified to begin with'.
2. The Belfast example also draws on the language of outsiders and insiders. As Parker soon found out 'to be neither is not sufficient'. Your identity is, if you like, constructed in terms of what you are not; identity is marked by difference.
3. In both extracts we see the way we search for clues to locate people. In the Parker extract names and accents can give off contradictory messages. People's identities are defined in terms of names, accents and where they live, by culture, by meaning.

It is very important to note that the cultures and meanings that have generated divisions and conflicts within Belfast do not ultimately depend on issues about Belfast alone – they derive from a much broader conflict. And the divisions are primarily the result of the conflicting allegiances and identities of the two communities in Belfast to different nations – Britain and Ireland.

We'll come back to the issue of nations in Section 4.2 below. Before we do, we want to spend a short time thinking through one of the central concerns of this chapter: *culture* and its relationship to identity.

4.1.1 Culture and cultural analysis

You have already come across the idea of culture in a number of places and guises in DD100, for example:

- The concept of *sub-cultures* and their relationship to crime in Section 4.4 of the *Introductory Chapter*.
- Culture as a key social structure shaping identity in Chapter 1, Section 4.2 of *Questioning Identity*.
- The role of culture and meaning in relation to poverty and identity in Chapter 3 of *Questioning Identity*.
- Symbols and representations are important aspects of culture, Chapter 1, Section 8, *Questioning Identity*.

You will come across the notion of culture throughout DD100, so it is worth pausing for a moment to unpack the term.

What do you understand by the term culture (skim through your notes if you want to)?

You might have come up with something like:

ideas

art

language

beliefs

sub-cultures

popular culture

The concept of culture, as it is used in the social sciences, can encompass all of these things because at its broadest it refers to the realm of meaning – and meaning can and is produced in everyday conversations, in great works of art, by religious beliefs and rituals, etc.

Social scientists, without assuming any one type of culture is better or more meaningful than another or more worthy of investigation than another, recognize that there is a great diversity of cultures, realms of meaning and belief in any one society, and that these cultures cluster around specific social groups and social practices. *High culture* is the domain of traditional and elite art forms; *popular culture* is the realm of mass consumption and commodified culture. *Dominant cultures* reflect the meanings of the powerful; *sub-cultures* reflect the meanings of the deviant or the marginal.

Given this range of meanings, what kinds of connections might there be between culture and identity?

This is a complex question, but you might bear some of the following in mind as you work through Chapter 4 and as you draw together materials from across Block 1.

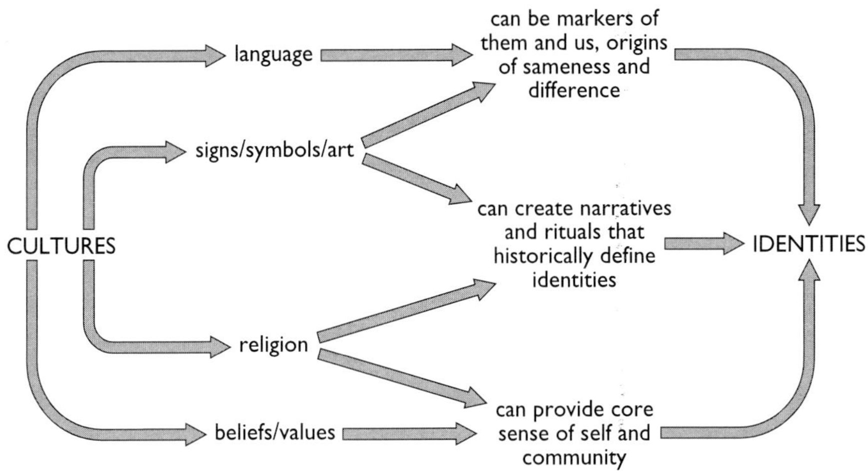

The task now is to use this general model to investigate the relationship between culture and national identity.

WORKBOOK ACTIVITY 4.2

Look over your notes on Sections 3 and 4 of Chapter 4. What role has culture, in all its forms, played in the formation of British national identity? What other social forces and processes have been involved?

COMMENT

In Section 3 the one unambiguous cultural pillar of Britishness was Protestantism – though the impact of this cannot be completely separated from fighting wars against Catholic states or the institutions of the Church of England. Section 4 deals with more explicitly cultural elements of Britishness: civil rituals and national symbols.

Perhaps the key point to take away is that all of these cultural phenomena which shape and represent British national identity have been created in the context of geographical factors (Britain as an island), military factors (empire building), and economic factors (industrialization and early prosperity). The division between political institution and cultural symbol is spanned by the role of the monarchy.

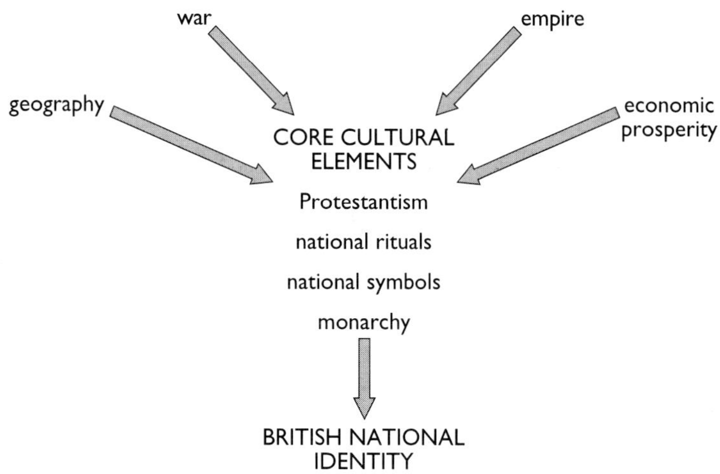

4.2 Concepts and theories: states, nations, nation-states

Our account of cultural and non-cultural factors in the shaping of British national identity leaves open the question of quite how cultural structures interact with and are shaped by politics, military affairs, economics, geography, etc. To open up these issues, we need some sharper concepts and more explicit theories – the core elements of constructing a social science argument.

Section 2 of Chapter 4 used these concepts and theories.

Key concepts	Key theories
State	Gellner
Nation	Anderson
Nation-state	Smith
Nationalism	

WORKBOOK ACTIVITY 4.3

Read over your notes on the four key concepts. How might we diagrammatically represent their interrelationships?

Are any of the concepts primarily cultural phenomena?

COMMENT

We came up with the following diagram.

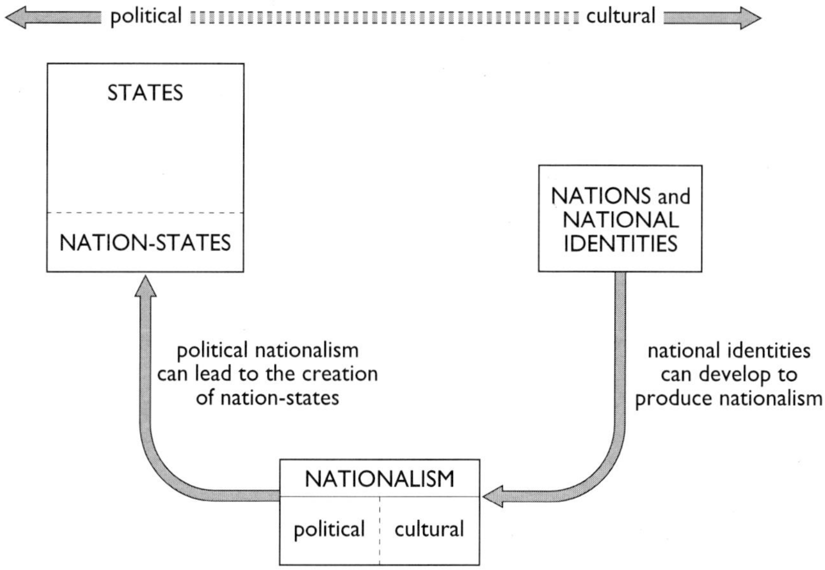

We would argue that states and nation-states are primarily political–legal phenomena. Both are rule-making institutions, nation-states being that subset of states which have fixed borders and homogenous internal rule.

Nations are primarily cultural phenomena – social groups bound by a shared identity rooted in shared histories.

Nationalism is both cultural and political: cultural in that it describes a cluster of attitudes and beliefs about a nation; political in that these attitudes often contribute to a political project to obtain self-rule or an independent nation-state for that nation.

Not surprisingly the above diagram leaves a lot unsaid. For example:

1 How do states and why do states get turned into nation-states?

2 What happens to those people who live within the territory of a nation-state, but do not share the identity of the nation?

3 Where did nations come from in the first place?

We can represent this list of issues by amending our original diagram with corresponding numbers.

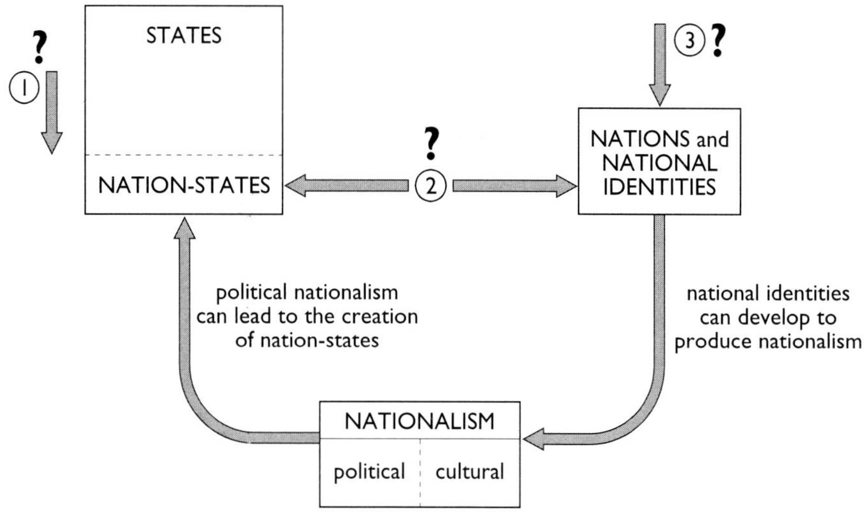

Different theories approach these issues in different ways. So, let's look at some theory.

WORKBOOK ACTIVITY 4.4

Look back over your notes to Section 2.2 and have a go at filling in the grid below.

Three theories of nations

Theorist	Origins of nation-states Key claims	Origins of nations Key claims	Fate of other cultures and identities Key claims
Gellner			
Anderson			
Smith			

COMMENT

If you're having trouble with this, think through the following sketches of the three theorists' core arguments.

The focus of Gellner's theory is on the origin of nations and national identities and the fate of peripheral nations.

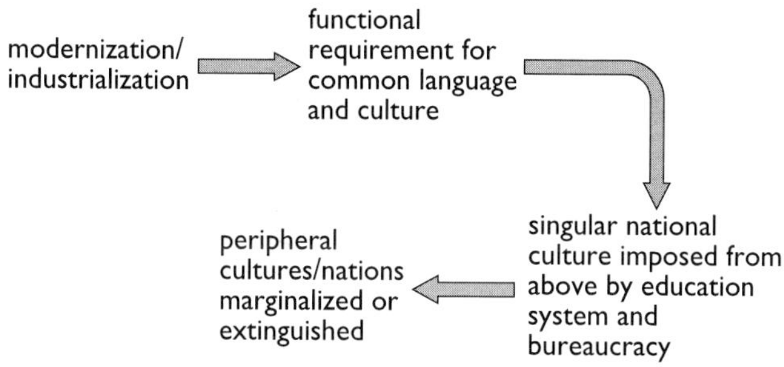

Anderson's theory touches on the origins of nation-states, but has more to say about the origins of nations.

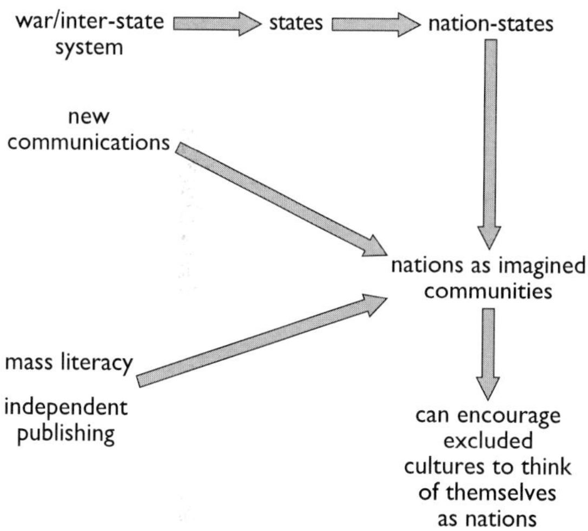

Smith's theory, unlike Gellner's and Anderson's, is most focused on the origins of nations. He agrees that imposed cultures and imagining must begin with a pre-existing ethnic core. Nations cannot be invented out of nowhere and nothing.

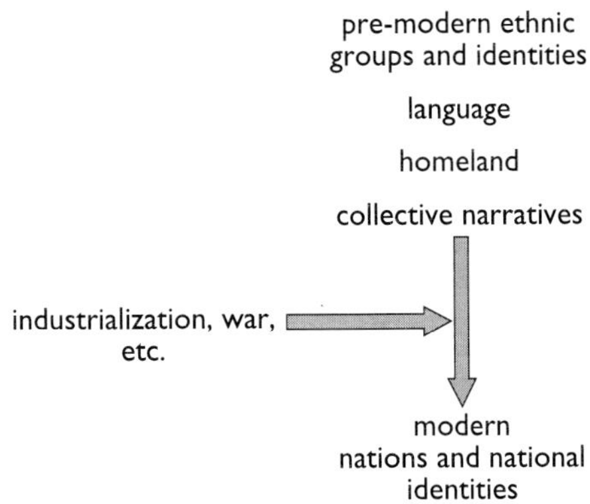

The point here is not to evaluate which theory is strongest – you will be doing a lot more of this in Blocks 4 and 5. At this stage we want you to note how theories animate, connect and use the same concepts, but emphasize different arguments and make different *claims* about the same subject.

Three theories of nations: completed grid

Theorist	Origins of nation-states Key claims	Origins of nations Key claims	Fate of other cultures and identities Key claims
Gellner		Imposed from above, by nation-building state elites	Peripheral cultures quashed. Folk cultures eradicated
Anderson	War and inter-state system	Imagined by elites and new mass literate politics	Can lead to peripheral nationalism
Smith	War and inter-state system	Must begin from pre-modern ethnic cores or ethnies	

4.3 Reading visual evidence

Your work on this chapter and the rest of the book has involved not only reading words but looking at a whole range of other kinds of material: photos, posters, maps. Our experience tells us that students vary in their responses to this kind of material. Some pass it by quickly thinking it is the written word they need to concentrate on. Others may welcome it as a relief from a page of dense text, but do very little with it. Enthusiastic photographers or map readers perhaps may become very involved with these images. In this course we don't want you to pass over the visual images quickly. However, unless you fall into the third of our categories you may well need some more help in knowing just what to look for, how to read them and how to use them.

4.3.1 Reading images

Look at the photo in Figure 6. You will have come across it in Section 4 of Chapter 4.

The Remembrance Sunday ceremony is a ritual which presents people with part of the story of the British nation. It is part of the narrative of what it means to be British. Because of the coverage and attention given to the event each year it is a ceremony whose significance may be recognized and understood by many British people, even if they do not respond to it in the same way.

FIGURE 6 The Cenotaph, Whitehall on Remembrance Sunday

WORKBOOK ACTIVITY 4.5

1 What are the symbols used in the picture in Figure 6? List what you can see.

2 What meanings are attached to what you can see in the picture? What do you associate with your list in 1?

3 Finally, it is this photo, or one very like it, which appears in most newspapers in November. But could it have been constructed differently, with a different focus? What implications might this have for the meanings which are being communicated?

COMMENT

1 The kinds of words we came up with immediately were:

> flag, religion, the church, hierarchy, discipline, uniforms, men, spectacle, soldiers, grouping, differentiation, solidarity, a cross, armed forces

This list depends on some interpretations of symbols. For example, we have noted down both cross and religion. We needed to understand what a cross stands for before we could get to religion. And similarly we needed to be able to interpret guardsmen's hats to the right of the picture to give us armed forces.

2 Your response will depend on your own experience and on whether you are familiar with some of these military symbols. This image conveys a powerful message. In fact it conveys large elements of the five pillars of Britishness identified in Section 3 of Chapter 4. The message becomes more powerful once we introduce our own knowledge of the context of the ceremony. We could add: the two World Wars, the Gulf War, and the Falklands War. We could say more about the participants: heads of state of Commonwealth countries, the Queen, and the British Legion. We can also link the photo to the two minutes silence on the eleventh hour of the eleventh day of the eleventh month. The presence of dignitaries makes this a high-status occasion and an important ritual.

3 The photo is one you would expect to see of the Remembrance Sunday ceremony and it is constructed in such a way as to make sure the meanings we have picked up on are clear to people looking at it.

But it could have been constructed differently to convey different meanings:

- A focus on just one of the groups of participants, the Queen, for example, or a politician, would serve to emphasize this particular element in the national story.
- A close-up of disabled young service men would be emphasizing just one part of the narrative.
- The juxtaposition of this kind of image with one of a soldier selling his medals, or of a current protest about British military actions overseas would convey yet another message.

4.3.2 Reading maps

You will be using maps throughout DD100, and we will be looking at reading maps in much more detail in Block 4. But before we get there it is worth practising at extracting information from maps.

Below we have reproduced one of the maps from Chapter 4. Have another look at it, especially if you didn't find the maps useful when reading the chapter, and then do the activity below.

WORKBOOK ACTIVITY 4.6

Look at the map in Figure 7: what light, if any, does it shed on the following question?

- Is the idea of an authentic ethnic British, English or Scottish nation tenable?

COMMENT

The map shows that during this period the idea of a singular, unified ethnic British, Scottish or English person was unintelligible. Scotland barely exists as a meaningful entity, divided between Picts, Scandinavians, invading Scots (from the island of Ireland) and Anglo-Saxon settlement as far north as the Firth of Forth. Similarly, look at the area that you would now think of as England. The post-Roman occupants were overrun by Angles, Saxons and Jutes from the European mainland and, across a significant swath, overrun again by Scandinavians. The Norman Conquest meant that whoever it was that lived in what is now England acquired a French-speaking elite of Scandinavian origin.

FIGURE 7 One contemporary representation of post-Roman migrations and invasions during the period from 500 AD to the Norman Conquest in 1066

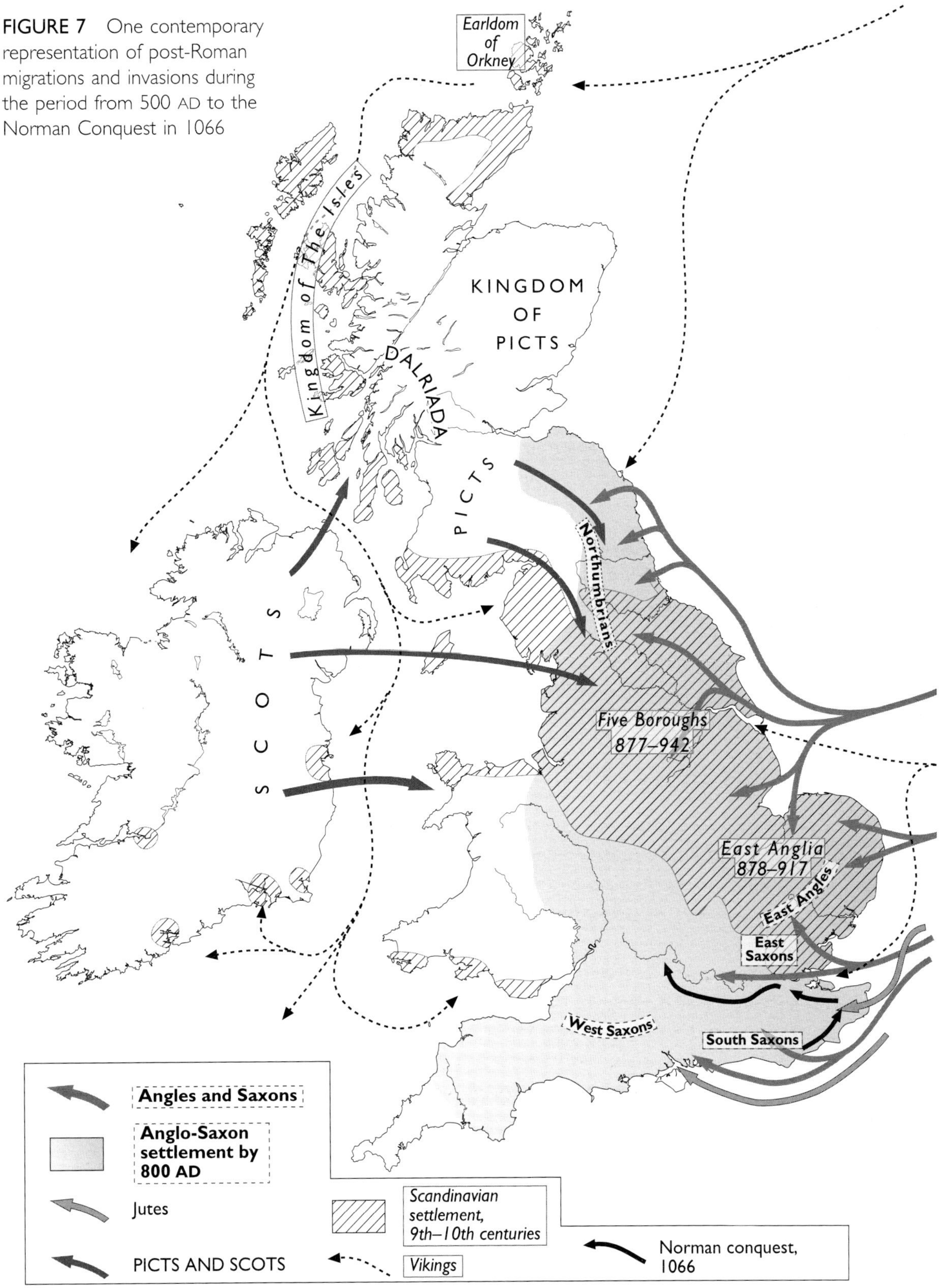

4.4 The argument of Chapter 4: how has it been constructed?

You will be aware that one of our tasks in this workbook has been to look at how social scientists put arguments together. Now it's your turn.

What we want you to do is to construct an argument to explain the rise of Scottish nationalism, that is, in response to the question:

What accounts for the recent rise of Scottish nationalism?

This task is very similar to one you will be asked to do for Part 1 of TMA 01. So you can see this as preparation for your next TMA.

We are going to construct an argument in response to this question, but we will do it in a series of stages. For each stage we will ask you to construct part of the argument, we will then give you our suggestion and a few comments on the skills we are using.

WORKBOOK ACTIVITY 4.7

The question asks about the rise of Scottish nationalism. So for an introductory paragraph we need to define the concept of nationalism in general and explain the Scottish case in particular, and we need to explain what we mean by 'rise'.

COMMENT

This is our suggestion:

In 1997 the Scottish people voted in favour of establishing a Scottish Parliament. The large majority for devolution and the significant minority for independence stood in marked contrast to earlier periods of Scottish history during which advocates of an unchanged Union were stronger and Britishness was a stronger component of Scot's identities. A Scottish nation, in the sense of a people with distinct civic institutions and shared culture, existed in elite form before the Union and became a mass popular nation afterwards. But this nation made little attempt to rule itself. We need to explain why identities in Scotland seem to be shifting from Britishness towards Scotishness and why the balance of political opinion has shifted from the Union to the more explicitly nationalist positions of devolution and independence.

What we have done in this first paragraph is define and contextualize what seems to be the key concepts – the *rise* in *Scottish nationalism.*

As you know, definitions can be a source of disagreement. But as long as we have set out clearly at the start what we understand by a particular concept and as long as we work with this throughout the argument then the work will be coherent.

WORKBOOK ACTIVITY 4.8

In Section 5.2 of Chapter 4 economic change, political marginalization and the role of the SNP are identified as three possible factors which may explain the rise in nationalism. These need to be dealt with in three separate paragraphs after your introduction.

Try writing out the first sentence for each of these paragraphs.

COMMENT

Here are our suggestions:

Paragraph 1

First, significant economic change in recent years means that Scotland now gains little economically as a result of its links with England.

Paragraph 2

Second, we need to consider political changes which have resulted in Scotland becoming increasingly separated and marginalized in relation to English politics.

Paragraph 3

Finally, the two changes outlined above have provided the opportunity for the SNP to increase and widen its support.

What we have here are three general statements, each progressing the argument.

The progression here is simple. The signposting words 'First', 'Second', and 'Finally' indicate that all three statements are taking the argument in the same kind of direction. Other signposting words we could have used are 'in addition', or 'moreover'. If we had wanted to signal a change in direction of our argument we would have used different words, such as 'on the other hand', 'alternatively', or 'however'. All these indicate a new and opposing idea. But to understand and to be able to think about these general statements a little more we need some examples, some evidence.

WORKBOOK ACTIVITY 4.9

So what happens inside a paragraph?

Let's look at the first paragraph on economic change. How are you going to follow that first sentence?

You may want to jot down some notes.

COMMENT

Our suggestion:

First, significant economic change in recent years means that Scotland now gains little economically as a result of its links with England. As part of Britain and its Empire, Scotland experienced prosperity, but from the First World War onwards this changed. Traditional industries such as coal and shipbuilding declined. In England these industries were replaced by new industries such as chemicals. This did not happen in Scotland. In recent years it was hoped that North Sea oil revenues would revive the Scottish economy, but some Scots are of the opinion that too many of these revenues have moved south. So there was an increasing feeling that Scotland would be better off economically going it alone.

The important point to note here is that inside a paragraph the points you make are supported by evidence and connected to the opening claim/ sentence of the paragraph. The paragraph is internally coherent. If you want to say something which does not agree with the first sentence then you need to start a new paragraph.

WORKBOOK ACTIVITY 4.10

So far we have presented a fairly straightforward argument using three of the factors identified in Section 5.2. We could close the argument by summarizing these three changes.

However, in Sections 5.2.3 and 5.2.4 of the chapter you are presented with a more complex argument. We want you to use the latter half of Section 5.2.3 (in which distinctions are made between civic nationalism and ethnic nationalism) and the arguments of Section 5.2.4 to bring the argument to a close. In effect, to begin writing a conclusion.

COMMENT

Here is our suggestion:

The argument presented so far has focused on economic and political factors in the rise of a singular Scottish nationalism. But what form will this nationalism take? What we are seeing emerging at present is civic nationalism: a shared allegiance to institutions and cultures. But the emergence of ethnic and exclusive nationalisms are still real if remote possibilities. So far, Scottish culture and politics has favoured the civic variant, it remains to be seen whether the spectre of ethnic nationalism will arise.

You probably realized that the final part of Section 5.2.3 is the one which raises the most questions about Scottish nationalism. What we have done here is only one suggestion. But can you see how it rounds off the argument by returning to the original definitions we were working with?

4.5 Using the course themes: problems of Englishness

In the Introductory Block you were introduced to the course themes of DD100 and one of the claims made for them was that they help you focus on important issues.

The case of England and English national identity explored in Chapter 4, Section 6 draws on the themes of *uncertainty and diversity* and *structure and agency*. As a final activity on Chapter 4 we want you to work through Section 6 with these themes in mind.

WORKBOOK ACTIVITY 4.11

How do the first two sub-sections of Section 6 use the ideas of uncertainty and diversity? Make brief notes.

COMMENT

Section 6.1

devolution/decolonization → uncertainty about Britishness
post-war migration → exposes Englishness

Englishness – roots in declining aristocratic class, therefore *uncertainty* about contemporary English identity.

Diverse alternative Englands possible – but uncertain if they can capture national mood.

Section 6.2

Black immigration makes Englishness as whiteness an untenable and racist source of national identity.

Possibly uncertainty about Englishness will decline if it can embrace diversity.

WORKBOOK ACTIVITY 4.12

How does Section 6.3 and the discussion of English nationalism draw upon notions of structure and agency?

COMMENT

1 Uncertainties about Englishness have structural origins beyond the control of individuals or social groups, i.e. devolution, Europe, etc.

2 Absence of specifically English structures – like civic institutions – makes construction of Englishness problematic.

3 Popular/media agency has alighted on English football as an alternative. Some, for example Weight, claim appropriation of St. George's flag helps actively foster alternative popular inclusive English nationalism.

5 CONSOLIDATION AND REFLECTION

As with the Introductory Block, we are going to round off our work on Block 1 by consolidating and reflecting on the materials we have worked through. The Afterword to *Questioning Identity* (as with subsequent books on DD100) begins the process of consolidation. Then the TV programme and Audio-cassette 3, Side B, give you more of a chance to reflect upon and explore some key issues in the block.

▶ **Now read Kath Woodward's Afterword in *Questioning Identity* and return to this point in the workbook.**

We hope you are beginning to establish for yourself what the most useful form of consolidation is for you.

One strategy might be to organize and condense your notes around a grid – look back to the Introduction of this workbook (p.9) where we set out one possible device for organizing your study of the chapters, based on the framing questions of the block.

Another closely related task would be to focus on two of the course themes (as we did in Section 4.5 of the workbook) – *uncertainty and diversity* and *structure and agency*. This is what we will do using the following grid.

WORKBOOK ACTIVITY 5.1

Try condensing some of your notes on a chapter by chapter basis on to the following grid – our version is at the back of the workbook.

▶ Now please listen to Audio-cassette 3, Side B and read the associated notes.

Also watch TV 01: *Defining Moments* and read the associated notes. Please check the *Study Calendar* for broadcast times.

Themes of Block 1

	What uncertainties are explored in this chapter?	Why is diversity important in understanding these uncertainties?	How do we see people in this chapter shaping their identities?	What structures constrain and generate control over our identities?
Chapter 2				
Chapter 3				
Chapter 4				

6 STUDY SKILLS: USING TUTORIALS, THE PHONE AND SELF-HELP GROUPS

So far the emphasis has been on you, as an individual student, working by yourself with the course materials. However, you are not expected to work with the materials all by yourself unless that is really your choice. Even then there will still be quite intensive communications with your tutor in relation to your assignments. Learning from your assignments was touched on in Section 8.1 of the *Introductory Workbook* and is covered in more depth in *Workbook 2*.

What about the other kinds of support that are available to you as you work through the course and how can you be sure you are making the most of them?

Look at these four scenarios. Read each one and note down your response.

Scenario 1

You are slowly falling behind with your work on Block 1. You still haven't read Chapter 4 and you should be starting on TMA 01. There is a tutorial tomorrow. Should you go to it or spend the time catching up?

Scenario 2

You really don't understand part of Chapter 3. You have gone over it again and again and you can't see what Weber meant by a status group and now you realize part of the TMA is about this. Should you phone your tutor to ask for some advice or will this be wasting her time? You know she is very busy.

Scenario 3

At the first tutorial you found that one of the other students lives in the next road to yours. He suggests getting together to discuss the next TMA but you are worried that this might count as cheating. Will it?

Scenario 4

You know you are not going to be able to get to tutorials. Does this mean you should not have started the course or that the OU is the wrong place for you?

We want to start with scenario 4 because it is important to hear that the OU is committed to enabling people who would not be able to attend a conventional university to get degrees – so if you are not able to get to tutorials you must not let this deter you. We know that for some students attendance is not possible. If you are one of these students, your tutor will be able to put you in touch with other students studying the same course who may live near or be able to telephone you. You will be encouraged to keep in touch with the tutor yourself by telephone or letter, for students with disabilities special support can be arranged through your OU regional office.

Our response to scenario 1 would be that you should try to get to the tutorial. You will find that you are not the only person who is struggling to keep up. Your tutor will be ready for this and will be able to suggest ways of catching up. Let your tutor know of any difficulties. You will probably find that once you have mentioned a problem like this everyone else chimes in to agree with you. Don't be put off if some people in the group seem on top of their work. OU students vary enormously in terms of their educational experiences before starting a course and the time they have available to study the course. Remember, tutorials are not lectures. Come prepared to argue and ask questions, and listen to others. Doing this kind of work, often in small groups, leads to far better understanding and remembering, but it can take some getting used to.

If you are having a difficulty like the one in scenario 2, it is very important to phone your tutor. An important part of his or her job is to help students over the phone There are a few ground rules that will make this work better:

- if your tutor has told you already when are good times to phone, try to stick to these
- make some notes on the difficulty before you call, so that you can explain it clearly
- if you start getting confused whilst on the phone, and working like this does need a lot of concentration, ask the tutor if you can phone back when you have digested where you have got to.

With regard to scenario 3, discussing your TMA with another student can be very helpful indeed and certainly is not cheating. Your tutor will probably be encouraging you to form self-help groups: self-help can take the form of just calling each other for moral support but if you arrange meetings, try to have a definite topic to discuss. Remember though that when it comes to finally writing your TMA, the work must be all your own. This should not be a problem. Everyone has different ways of working through the ideas you have discussed. It is very difficult to produce the same piece of work as someone else.

7 ASSESSING BLOCK 1

It is now time to think about writing TMA 01. You have already covered a lot of ground on writing skills and learning from assessment.

- In the *Introductory Workbook*, Section 8, we covered the purpose of assessments (to help you understand the course) and the role of the workbooks in this (practising the skills you are assessed on).
- Section 1.3 of this workbook, as well as TMA 07, have given you a chance to practise writing.
- Section 1.3 also covered some basic ground rules for successful writing, and Section 8.4 of the *Introductory Workbook* introduced you to ways of referencing your writing.

In this section of the workbook we begin by answering some frequently asked questions about writing in the OU (Section 7.1), cover some guidelines for preparing to write (Section 7.2), and look at a few key points on the structure and purpose of TMA 01 (Section 7.3).

7.1 Frequently asked questions about essay writing for your TMAs

How closely do I need to follow the student notes? What if I want to answer the questions differently?

You received quite firm advice in the *Introductory Workbook* about using the student notes. In the early stages of the course, in particular, these notes will be detailed and will spell out for you very fully how to approach the question. If you find yourself wanting to do something very different it would probably be a good idea to stop and phone your tutor.

What kind of language should I be trying to use? Something like the language which is used in the chapters? Will this count as copying?

Another way of putting this might be: how can I manage to write in what sounds like an academic way without almost copying from the chapter?

This is not easy and it doesn't help to say it will come with practise. What you write can sound, as we have heard one student express it, very 'Janet and Johnish' compared to what members of the course team have written. Certainly if you are not sure exactly what something means it is easier to use the words in the chapter. However, copying is never acceptable and your tutor will warn you about this if it occurs. If you use the words of someone else you must reference them. Talking about the course ideas, as much as you can, to anyone who will listen – not just fellow students – and engaging with the ideas of the course will help you become more confident in using the language of the social sciences.

What about my own opinions and ideas? Can they be brought in at all?

Of course your own ideas and views are important: they will help you to engage with the course material. Using and testing those ideas are part of becoming an active and independent learner. The key issue is to subject your ideas and opinions to the same rigorous analysis we expect of social science arguments. You have already seen during your work on Block 1 that constructing and evaluating an argument in the social sciences involves quite specific components: clearly stated claims, systematic use of a range of evidence, clarity of concepts, etc. This can result in quite a different approach to issues and even a different style of writing from some kinds of journalism or from a discussion with friends or family. You may well find that an assignment task involves you in presenting an argument about something you have strong views on. You will need to construct the argument carefully, as a social scientist. You will need to pay attention to definitions, supporting evidence and internal coherence rather than relying on appeals to, for example, 'common sense' or what is 'natural'.

7.2 Preparing to write an essay

In Section 1.3 of this workbook you had a chance to practise writing skills and look at some key guidelines for good writing: use your own words, answer the question, organize your material, and use the conventional structure of introduction, main section, conclusion and references. In this section we will move on to how to actually organize yourself to achieve these ends. The key is planning.

Thorough preparation and planning is the basis of any good piece of written work. Here are some reminders for those of you already experienced in essay planning, and some suggestions for anyone coming to OU social science essay writing for the first time.

1 Look back

- If this is not your first essay, and if you haven't done so already, take a look at your previous one. Did your tutor make any suggestions that you need to bear in mind for this essay? Did you learn anything else about essay writing?

2 Read the question

- Identify the process or 'command' words like, *discuss, evaluate, explore.* These tell you how you have to answer the question. A list of these words and their definitions are covered in the Appendix at the end of this workbook.
- Identify the 'content' words. These tell you what you have to write about.
- Let's consider the question:

  Identities in the contemporary UK are becoming more uncertain. Discuss.

  'Discuss' is the command word. It implies that you have to explore the evidence for and against the statement. The content words are 'the contemporary UK' and 'uncertain'. So, the evidence that you need to explore should focus on whether there is increasing uncertainty about identities in Britain and you need to ask what 'uncertainty' might mean in this context.

3 Identify the relevant material

- Read the guidance notes that you get with each question. These will prevent a lot of unnecessary suffering and should always be consulted.

4 Organize the material

- Options include 'brainstorming' your ideas for the essay on paper: jot down a list of questions and issues prompted by the questions, all the relevant examples you can think of and any other related evidence; re-check notes and add left-out material; and then link connected ideas and points.
- Collate and write out these points on separate sheets of paper, on 'post-it notes', or on index cards.
- Shuffle these until you've got them in a logical order. **This is your essay plan**.
- Ideas may come to you at unexpected moments – for these keep a notebook handy and jot them down.

5 First draft to final version

- Working from your essay plan, begin writing a first draft. You may need to revise your plan as the essay takes shape. Don't worry, this is perfectly normal!
- Do the best you can, but see it as a first draft and expect to make some improvements. You may even want to prepare a second draft before writing the final version.
- We all know that people sometimes put their first draft straight in the post. If you have time, always put the essay aside for at least a day to let the dust settle, show it to a friend or another student to get feedback, and

then re-read the question and the essay yourself. Its strengths and weaknesses should now be a lot clearer to you.

- You're now in a position to write your definitive answer. Now is the time to consider more carefully your presentation (sentence structure, grammar, etc.) and to check for clarity of expression.
- When this is complete, fill in your PT3 form, put the whole lot in the post and await your tutor's comments with quiet confidence.

In *Workbook 2* we will offer you more detailed help through the process of first draft to final version.

SUMMARY

Essay planning has five principal stages:

- Reading and understanding the question.
- Identifying the relevant material.
- Making an essay plan.
- Writing a first draft.
- Reviewing the first draft and writing a final version.

7.3 TMA 01

TMA 01 is different each year, but it will have the same format and aims. You will find the question for this year with detailed advice in your *Assignment Booklet 1*. In this section we want to help you to think about the TMA and to show you how each section of this workbook has helped prepare you for doing it.

The first part of the TMA is asking you to show that you understand what is meant in social science by concepts, theories and explanations, evidence, etc., and the way these are brought together to form an argument.

The second part of the TMA is where you are asked to present an argument yourself using all these components. This is what you will already have practised in relation to your work on Chapter 4. So, again, you will have an example to work from.

The third part of the TMA is exactly the same as it was for TMA 07: a short exercise in self-assessment. You may find it useful to return to Section 8.3 of the *Introductory Workbook* to remind yourself of this exercise.

The subject matter of the TMA is, of course, about identity, but it is also asking you quite explicitly to show that you are able to use the skills we have been concentrating on in this first block, that is, how social scientists construct arguments. The figure below provides a summary of the way in which you have been building up these skills throughout your work on *Workbook 1*.

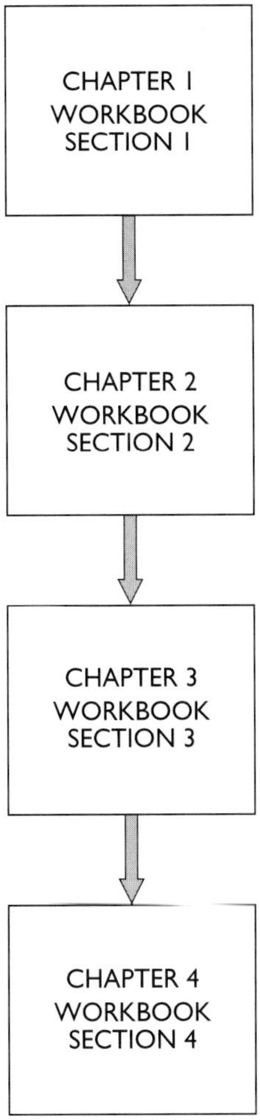

Using general concepts to bring together many particular examples.

Using concepts to generate theories to generate explanations.

i.e. Mead, Freud and Goffman.

Breaking down a social science argument into core claims and clarifying their interconnections.

i.e. the account of Murphy and Elwood of gender performance in schools.

Comparing and contrasting arguments.

i.e. Marx versus Weber, class versus consumption.

Combining arguments.

i.e. accounts of the origins of uncertainty in economic identities.

Using and comparing theories.

i.e. Gellner, Anderson and Smith.

Supporting key claims with evidence, concluding an argument.

i.e. accounting for the rise of Scottish nationalism.

FIGURE 8 Skills diagram: constructing social science arguments in Block 1

You can now get started on TMA 01. Good luck.

Please turn to *Assignment Booklet 1* for TMA 01.

COMMENT ON WORKBOOK ACTIVITY 3.6

Marx and Weber: completed grid

	Marx	Weber
What is the structural basis of class divisions?	Ownership and non-ownership of capital: the means of production	Market position, access to or possession of wealth, qualifications, skills
Is class the main division in society?	Yes – economic divisions are replicated by political and cultural divisions	No – class divisions are cross-cut with status and power
How many classes are there in capitalist societies?	Two – the bourgeoisie or ruling class and the working class	Many – dependent upon the structure of the labour market: types of job, demand for skills, etc.
What relationship exists between classes?	Mutually interdependent, but locked into unequal conflict	Variety of relationships possible: hierarchies of power and deference, inter-class competition or alliances, sometimes conflict
How and under what conditions do class divisions generate identities?	When class consciousness is recognized. Class identity emerges through polarization of economic conditions, collective agency and struggle	Class only one component of identity. Most identities spring from status groups but organized collective action is also important

COMMENT ON WORKBOOK ACTIVITY 5.1

Themes of Block 1: completed grid

	What uncertainties are explored in this chapter?	Why is diversity important in understanding these uncertainties?	How do we see people in this chapter shaping their identities?	What structures constrain and generate control over our identities?
Chapter 2	Gendered identities becoming uncertain, limits of essentialist categories make for uncertainty.	Individuals possess adverse and sometimes contradictory range of gendered characteristics. The fuzzy nature of gendered identities makes diversity possible.	Children actively identifying with socially constructed categories.	School teachers' expectations, family life, biological and cognitive structures.
Chapter 3	Economic identities like class becoming uncertain as work changes.	Complexity of new patterns of work and consumption lead to uncertainty.	The poor reject identities imposed on them. Classes organize around and can entrench identity.	Inequalities of wealth and power.
Chapter 4	Uncertainties around Britishness and English national identity.	Devolution, immigration and European Union offer diverse identities which may conflict with and undermine old identities.	Scots shifting to a more nationalist less British identity.	Historically rooted national cultures and conflicts. Ceremonies and historical narratives.

APPENDIX: PROCESS AND COMMAND WORDS IN ESSAY QUESTIONS

Account for	Explain, clarify, give reasons for.
Analyse	Resolve into its component parts. Examine critically or minutely.
Assess	Determine the value of, weigh up (see also Evaluate).
Compare	Look for similarities and differences between, perhaps reach conclusions about which is preferable and justify this clearly.
Contrast	Set in opposition in order to bring out the differences sharply.
Compare and contrast	Find some points of common ground between x and y and show where or how they differ.
Criticize	Make a judgement (backed by a discussion of the evidence or reasoning involved) about the merit of theories or opinions or about the truth of facts.
Define	State the exact meaning of a word or phrase. In some cases it may be necessary or desirable to examine different possible or often used definitions.
Describe	Give a detailed account of ...
Discuss	Explain, then give two sides of the issue and any implications.
Distinguish or differentiate between	Look for differences between ...
Evaluate	Make an appraisal of the worth/validity/effectiveness of something in the light of its truth or usefulness (see also Assess).
Examine the argument that ...	Look in detail at this line of argument.
Explain	Give details about how and why it is ...
How far ...	To what extent ... Usually involves looking at evidence/ arguments for and against and weighing them up.
Illustrate	Make clear and explicit, usually requires the use of carefully chosen examples.
Justify	Show adequate grounds for decisions or conclusions, answer the main objections likely to be made about them.

Outline	Give the main features or general principles of a subject, omitting minor details and emphasizing structure and arrangement.
State	Present in a brief, clear way.
Summarize	Give a concise, clear explanation or account of ... presenting the chief factors and omitting minor details and examples (see also Outline).
What arguments can be made for and against the view that ...	Look at both sides of this argument.

Source: Redman, P. *et al.* (1998) *Good Essay Writing: A Social Sciences Guide*, Milton Keynes, The Open University, pp.66–7.

ACKNOWLEDGEMENTS

Grateful acknowledgement is made to the following sources for permission to reproduce material in this workbook.

Figures

Figure 5: Bright, M., 'Boys performing badly', *The Observer*, 4 January 1998, © *The Observer* 1998; Figure 6: Popperfoto.

Cover

Image copyright © 1996 PhotoDisc, Inc.

STUDY SKILLS INDEX

IWB = *Introductory Workbook*
WB1 = *Workbook 1*

abbreviations, note taking, 21 (IWB)
active reading, 15 (IWB)
active reading and note taking, 19 (IWB)
adaptable reading strategies, 16 (IWB)
assessing Block 1, 64 (WB1)
assessment, benefits, 48 (IWB)
averages, 35 (WB1)
averages, rule for calculating, 35 (WB1)

Block 1: *Questioning Identity*, 39 (IWB)
Block 2: *The Natural and the Social*, 39 (IWB)
Block 3: *Ordering Lives*, 40 (IWB)
Block 4: *A Globalizing World?*, 40 (IWB)
Block 5: *Knowledge and the Social Sciences*, 41 (IWB)
blocks and course themes, 38 (IWB)

circuit of knowledge, 16 (WB1)
concepts, 11 (WB1)
concepts and theories, 46 (WB1)
consolidating, 46 (IWB), 60 (WB1)
constructing a social science argument, 12, 27, 55 (WB1)
course study calendar, 44 (IWB)
course themes, 35 (IWB)

essay questions, process and command words, 71 (WB1)
essay writing, four golden rules, 14 (WB1)
essays, inside a paragraph, 57 (WB1)
essays, introductory paragraph, 55 (WB1)
essays, preparing to write, 65 (WB1)
essays, what a social science essay looks like, 15 (WB1)
essays for TMAs, frequently asked questions, 64 (WB1)
evaluation, 17 (WB1)
extracting, 19, 22 (IWB)

facts and data, referenced as, 53 (IWB)
focused reading, 17 (IWB)

Harvard system for referencing, 54 (IWB)

identifying, 19 (IWB)
independent learner, 13 (IWB)

median, 36 (WB1)

percentages, 24 (WB1)
percentages, comparing, 34 (WB1)
percentages, rule for calculating, 25 (WB1)
plagiarism, 15 (WB1)
planning, time and tasks, 11 (IWB)
processing, 19, 23 (IWB)

quotations, referenced as, 53 (IWB)

reading bar charts, 26 (WB1)
reading images, 51 (WB1)
reading maps, 53 (WB1)
reading visual evidence, 50 (WB1)
references, at the end of a TMA, 54 (IWB)
references, in the text, 53 (IWB)
referencing, 53 (IWB)
re-presenting, 19, 23 (IWB)

scan, 17 (IWB)
self-evaluation questions, 52 (IWB)
self-help groups, 13 (IWB)
self-help groups, use of, 62 (WB1)
signposting words, 56 (WB1)
skim, 17 (IWB)
students, support from, 13 (IWB)
students with disabilities, special support, 63 (WB1)

tabular notes, 31 (IWB)
telephone, use of, 62 (WB1)
telephoning your tutor, ground rules, 63 (WB1)
theories, 12 (WB1)
tutorials, use of, 62 (WB1)
tutors, support from, 12 (IWB)

writing skills, 14 (WB1)